The Transcriber's Art

Selected Articles from Soundboard 1996–2006

by
Richard Yates

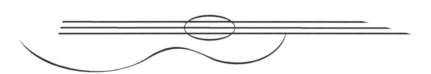

1 2 3 4 5 6 7 8 9 0

Visit us on the Web at www.melbay.com or billsmusicshelf.com

Contents

Preface

In the summer of 1995, *Soundboard* Editor-in-Chief Peter Danner wrote, "Your editor is curious to know what percentage of our readers play or otherwise use the music contained in *Soundboard* ... We are anxious to know if this material is of interest. We welcome suggestions and contributions of suitable music for future publication."

With a hodgepodge of transcriptions in various stages of completion, I wrote to Peter and submitted the first piece in what was to become a 10-year series of articles about guitar transcription of music originally written for other instruments.

My original intent was for the series to be an interactive forum and rely heavily on other people's submissions. The acceleration in the rate of communication through the Internet soon meant that a quarterly publication was too infrequent for this part of the plan. However, many readers did step up and send in scores. In retrospect, the first was probably the most historic and helped the series gain acceptance. This was Stanley Yates' arrangement of the *Allemande* from Johann Sebastian Bach's second cello suite shortly before publication of his landmark volume of all six suites.

Other contributors over the years have enriched the series with splendid music using a variety of approaches.

Louis Romao—*The Merry Farmer*, Robert Schumann

Bill Scheel—*Largo* from *Harpsichord Sonata #5*, J. S. Bach

Michael Patilla—*Prelude #6*, Frédéric Chopin, and *Verso III*, Domenico Zipoli

James Katzenberger—*Sarabande* from *Partita, BWV 825*, J. S. Bach

Spencer Doidge—*Carioca*, Ernesto Nazareth

Dmitri Bachovich—*Berceuse Héroique*, Claude Debussy

Anthony Catalano—*Vénitienne*, Jean-Philippe Rameau

Although their contributions are not in this collection—lack of space, time and contact information have prevented that—their work is in issues of *Soundboard* available from the Guitar Foundation of America.

The change in editors to Richard M. Long in the fall of 2001 only continued the gratifying support for the series.

I had naively thought that producing this collection would be a simple matter of cutting and pasting old files together but had forgotten that those files were created in eight different versions of music-scoring software and using different engraving styles. As I rewrote text I also needed thorough, professional editing and I am indebted to Nadene LeCheminant for her effort and expertise with the words as well as with the graphic design.

Richard Yates, November 2008

Prelude 13
J. S. Bach

Throughout the history of the guitar, players have searched for ways to add to the repertoire through the transcription of music written for other instruments. Some of the results of these searches are legendary. The story of Andrés Segovia's performance of the Bach *Chaconne* is a well known highlight that helped establish the legitimacy of transcription. As significant as this was, it was only one event in a much longer history. Indeed, the earliest written instrumental music includes transcriptions of vocal works. Although not a direct ancestor of the guitar, the Renaissance lute was often used to perform such music. Collections of lute music from the 16th century by such outstanding composers and players as Francesco da Milano include original works as well as intabulations (transcriptions) of the vocal music of the time. This noble tradition has continued to the present day, and now a significant proportion of our repertoire was originally written for other instruments.

This article begins a series that will explore the process of transcription for performance on the guitar. It is intended to be an interactive column that relies heavily on readers' ideas, suggestions, questions, and contributions. Each issue will include both a complete transcription and readers' reactions to the previous issue's piece. In this way the column can be a forum for discussion of ideas, a source of music for players, a teaching tool, and a way for guitarists to cooperatively expand the literature of our instrument.

Before describing this issue's selection, a few words about my own assumptions are in order. First, I believe that all guitarists are transcribers. We all change the fingerings that are in published music and make countless editorial decisions about unspecified details. Who of us has not looked at some measure of music and thought "Why in the world would anyone try to play it that way?" and then re-fingered or re-arranged as we thought best. Second, there are many equally valid transcriptions. Editing decisions involve weighing many trade-offs, both technical and musical. The "best" solution is different for each player and depends on ability, strength, size, experience, and performance setting, as well as highly individualized inspiration, appreciation and expression of musical ideas. Although we are clearly emerging from the period in which "My way is the only way" was drilled into students, we should still strive to promote the idea that real music is ultimately individual and personal and so is based on the individual player's decisions about what is best for him or her. This cannot come from rigid rules and formulae, but is ideally based on a conscious consideration of all of the factors involved. Exchange of ideas among players will raise awareness of these factors, the decisions that we all already make, and their effect on the sounds that we produce. Of course, these two assumptions are also open for discussion. Remember, this is your column, and your opinions and ideas are both valid and valued.

This issue's transcription is J. S. Bach's *Prelude 13* from *The Well-Tempered Clavier, Book 1*. The collection of preludes and fugues from which this is taken was written for a keyboard instrument and was completed in 1722. What was the process by which this particular transcription was produced? As with most transcriptions, it required many choices among alternate solutions. I will focus only on those that illustrate some my own ideas about transcription, and which I hope will be of interest to readers.

The selection of a piece from *The Well-Tempered Clavier* requires little explanation. J. S. Bach is certainly both a giant in music history and a source of a great many successful guitar transcriptions. Are there any guitarists who have not played a piece by Bach? The first prelude—in C major—from this collection, is familiar to most players, but are there others that might sit well on the guitar? Surely these musical monuments have been examined extensively by guitarists, but, for me, there is an added excitement in discovering transcriptions where others have already looked. Such is the case with the featured prelude.

Initial considerations include tempo and texture. Pieces which comprise dense counterpoint or rely on a pianist's luxury of playing rapid passages with each hand simultaneously are unlikely candidates. Surveying *Prelude 13* shows

a reasonable tempo, an exclusively two-voice texture, and only half a measure of simultaneous sixteenth notes in each voice (more about this later). What about the range of pitch? In the original, the pitch range spans nearly four octaves. As is frequently the case with the transcription of Baroque keyboard music, the range will need to be compressed, usually by octave transposition of parts of the bass line. What of key selection? The original is in F sharp major, that is, six sharps! Not one of my favorites. By choosing the key of G major, the highest note will be a C# and we will have almost three octaves on the guitar to work with. So far, so good. Let's go ahead and start copying out the music in this key to see what other problems arise.

The first obstacle comes in the third measure when, on the fourth beat, the bass line drops to a D below the range of the guitar and we arrive at the first decision about compressing the range.

Figure 1

Moving bass notes up an octave is necessary and is usually not a problem if there is more than an octave distance between the two voices, but an important factor to consider is how moving part of the bass line will affect the continuity of the line. The scalewise descent of the bass line in this prelude is essential to the character of the piece as a whole and we should try to maintain it wherever possible. Happily, the first note that we

must contend with is not part of this scale, and when moved up an octave does not quite overlap the top voice. Similar considerations about transposing the bass line are required at several other points in the prelude. Would you do them differently?

One especially interesting spot is at measure 10, here transposed to G major.

Figure 2

In the original the bass line has been descending stepwise for two and a half measures when it suddenly leaps up a seventh and then continues down the scale again. It is as if Bach had to decide, just as we must in making a guitar transcription, where to break up the bass line so he would not run out of room.

Measure 13 presents a different problem. The original, again transposed to G major, is as follows.

Figure 3

This is not impossible. It is, however, rather difficult compared to most of the rest of the piece. The solution I have chosen is to simplify the bass line slightly, and it is, for me, the best trade-off musically and technically. It makes it possible to play the measure smoothly, leaves a bass line that is still coherent and convincing, and does not disrupt the harmonic progression. Some will undoubtedly disagree with this choice. What do you think? Measure 27 was originally:

Figure 4

I have chosen to leave out the pedal point on D and rewrite the top voice as two lines, consistent with the texture in the rest of the prelude. What are other possible solutions? Redo the whole piece with a dropped D tuning? Give up on the whole transcription? Move the top voice up an octave?

One last observation about this transcription concerns left-hand fingering. As with many of the preludes in this collection, this one is like a study that presents the player, whether of keyboard or guitar, with particular technical tasks. One of these is to maintain the continuity and character of the top voice, given the many large melodic leaps that it contains. This is mostly a matter of articulation. Allowing notes to ring past their written duration will detract from the line's melodic continuity. Fingering can and should facilitate the solution of this technical problem and the expression of this musical idea. For instance, in measure two the E in the top voice could be played on the open string. However, the sound would continue past and overlap the next note in the melody, an A. As I have fingered it, the E can be released before sounding the A and the interval is heard as a melodic one, as—I believe—was intended. In fact, the character of the piece seems to call for playing staccato many of these notes before leaps, and this is reflected in the fingering I chose in most, but not all, similar places. Notice that these characteristic melodic leaps occur both on and off the beat, and when articulated as I have described, produce a pleasant, bouncy, syncopated effect. Are there other views? How would you do it?

Perhaps you have strong opinions about other aspects of this transcription. Please send them in. What are your thoughts about transcription in general? Are there examples you would like to discuss? Have you produced transcriptions which you would like to share with other players? Would you like to see more transcriptions?

Prelude XIII
Well Tempered Clavier, Book 1

Transcribed for guitar
by Richard Yates

J. S. Bach
(1685–1750)

Allegretto

Wiegenlied

Franz Liszt

This is the second in a series of articles about transcribing music to play on the guitar. Reader comments and contributions are strongly encouraged.

An arrangement is "the adaptation of a composition for a medium different from that for which it was originally written, so made that the musical substance is essentially unchanged" (*Harvard Dictionary of Music, Second Edition*). Although the term "transcription" is sometimes used as a synonym for "arrangement," it also can imply a higher degree of fidelity to the original. Regardless of this distinction, the simple wording of the definition conceals complex and difficult ideas. What is "musical substance," after all? What is the "essence" that is to remain unchanged? We will find no easy answers to these questions, but the search teaches us much about music and its beauty. A transcription is successful to the extent that it preserves and expresses the essential musical substance of a composition. However, on rare occasions a transcription goes beyond this standard. Some transcriptions seem to grasp the essential musical substance as it existed in the intention of the composer and place it in a medium where the essence is expressed even more clearly than in the original form. Seeking and claiming knowledge of the intention of the composer sounds presumptuous, but is it not what is also necessary in performing music?

In general, the fewer changes made to the music in the course of making a transcription the better the chances are of preserving the musical essence. Accordingly, in searching for music that is suitable for guitar transcription, it would be well to keep in mind the technical and expressive strengths and limitations of the instrument. It is true that impressive guitar arrangements have been made of, for example, Beethoven symphony movements, but none would claim that the adaptations were easy ones or that nothing of substance was lost in the process.

The music of Franz Liszt would seem, on first consideration, to provide little that is useful for guitarists. Most of it is quite difficult on piano, an instrument which requires only one finger in order to play each note, let alone on guitar, which usually requires two. The pitch range often far exceeds the guitar's limits. Liszt used textures characteristic of the piano and its playing technique that are quite foreign to the guitar. It would be a mistake, however, to prematurely pass over his works. There is more to be found here than one would think.

It is common for composers' styles to change as they grow older. Particularly in those who live long lives, there is a tendency to produce works on a smaller scale and of a more introspective and intimate character as they age. This is true of Franz Liszt. In 1881, at the age of 70, he wrote the piano piece featured in this issue of *Soundboard*. It is a cradle song, or lullaby. Readers wishing to check other similar works for transcription sources should look for "*Wiegenlieder*" (German) or "*berceuses*" (French). The title alone suggests that it may be suitable for transcription. A cradle song presumably would be slow, soft, subtle, and intimate. These are musical qualities that the guitar is well suited to express. This piece in particular provides wonderful opportunities for drawing on the delicate variations of timbre of which the guitar is uniquely capable. These can only be indirectly suggested by the piano, but are part of the essential musical substance as I perceive it. Would Liszt approve? Again, we cannot know the answer to this, but we can look for clues to help us decide.

In his late works, Liszt continued to expand his harmonic vocabulary and explore beyond the known limits. He wrote that he wanted to "throw a lance as far as possible into the boundless realms of the future." As can be seen in pieces such as the *Cradle Song*, he achieves effects that strongly anticipate the impressionism of Debussy. Although small in scale and rarely heard (I could find no reference to recordings), the *Cradle Song* is remarkable both for its aesthetic qualities and for its place in the history of music. Liszt has reached the point where tonality begins to be ambiguous, and so the *Cradle Song* is rocking, dreamlike, drifting, and wistful. These are aspects of its essential musical substance to be preserved in transcription. In the original, the key signature has no sharps or flats. The choice of two flats as the key was made after several futile experiments, and was largely decided by the ease with which the bass line can be played (lots of open Ds and As), smoothly and with the capability to sustain the higher notes for their full duration. Indeed, I believe the effectiveness of this transcription is greatly helped by the ability to sustain notes—as originally written—in nearly all cases. This was a priority in fingering decisions. Some players may have difficulty sight-reading as the accidentals start piling up—look for a little surprise in measure 54. These difficulties will be quickly overcome as you become familiar with the piece; the technical demands are not great.

Aside from the transposition of the whole piece, no notes needed to be altered by octave transposition—a small miracle when transcribing piano music for guitar. Two difficult spots need mention. On measures 59 and 61 the trills originally extended for two measures each while the lower two lines continued beneath them. It is theoretically possible to do this on the guitar, but practically it is quite difficult. At least it is beyond my own capabilities; I would be glad to hear from any readers who are able to pull this off. Here is a suggested execution.

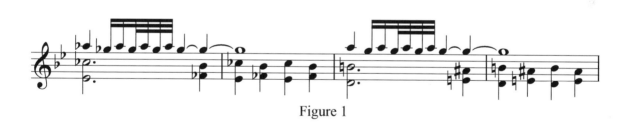

Figure 1

Does shortening these trills preserve the essential musical substance of the piece or is it a feeble makeshift that calls into question the legitimacy of the transcription? The answer to this and similar questions is ultimately a subjective one, but ideally is aided by reason and ideas that can be shared and discussed. What are your opinions of this transcription or the ideas expressed here about transcription? Have you made transcriptions that you would like others to try?

Wiegenlied

(Cradle Song)

Transcribed for guitar
by Richard Yates

Franz Liszt
(1811–1886)

To a Wild Rose

Edward MacDowell

Transcribing is not merely passing literally from one instrument to another. It means to find equivalents which change neither the aesthetic spirit nor the harmonic structure of the work being transcribed. —Andrés Segovia

In an earlier column I referred to the trade-offs that need to be considered in making transcriptions. Many decisions require careful assessment of the way the music is affected. This may include consideration of harmony, chord voicing, tone, playability, and articulation, as they affect what Segovia calls the "aesthetic spirit." It is usually not possible to maximize all of these factors. In making transcriptions we must often choose between preferred chord spacing and ease of execution or between sustaining notes for their full duration and ideal tone quality. This column will examine examples of these considerations using excerpts from a recently published transcription by Andrés Segovia.

It will be useful to first look more closely at the approach Segovia describes in the above quotation. In particular, the word "equivalents" is significant. It is clear that transcription requires changing some aspects of the original with the hope that these changes do not cause too large a distortion. What is not as obvious is that it is often necessary to make changes in order to preserve the original. In this context "equivalent" does not mean "the same." An example may help. The violin can produce sustained, legato sounds that can be continuously varied in volume; the guitar cannot. However, an equivalent that may sometimes be used is a guitar tremolo. This adds a great many notes in order to produce an effect that has an equivalence to the original. Considering the reverse transcription further illustrates

this point. Imagine making a violin transcription of a guitar tremolo piece such as Tarrega's *Recuerdos de la Alhambra.* Surely we would not ask the violinist to saw back and forth on dozens of little thirty-second notes, or make him really crank up his pizzicato, although we might find considerable amusement in his attempt. Rather, we would have him use the violin equivalent, a continuously bowed line.

The examples that we will use are from a transcription by Segovia of a well known piano piece by the American composer Edward MacDowell (1861–1908), titled *To a Wild Rose.* This has recently been published for the first time in *Guitar Review* magazine. The transcription is one piece in a collection of Segovia transcription manuscripts acquired last year by Yale University Music Library. Interested readers can find a facsimile of the manuscript and a performing score in the Winter 1996 edition of *Guitar Review.*

As we look at some of the specific changes that Segovia arrived at in his transcription we must keep in mind a couple of important points. First, our investigation of his reasons for particular choices will always be speculation. We have the original and the transcription, but no commentary by the transcriber. We must remember that this work was never published, although others in the same collection were. Whatever we infer cannot be verified, and there will always be other possible, non-musical explanations.

For instance, some of the differences we observe may simply be mistakes that would have been corrected before publication. The manuscript of this piece may have been a first draft simply to see if the piece warranted further investigation. I know that anyone perusing my own files would find a large number of incomplete, awkward, and error-filled attempts. Also, the transcription was made when Segovia was only 28 years old and may not represent the culmination of his thinking in this area. However, these limits to the validity of our investigation are not a real liability. Our purpose is not to do retrospective mind reading but to use the piece to show the types of considerations the transcriber must make.

A second caution must be made before we proceed. It is not the purpose of this analysis to make final judgments about which choices are best, but rather, to increase awareness of the variety of factors that should be weighed in making choices. How these different factors are judged is a subjective and personal matter.

One of the first diversions from the original score occurs in measure 4.

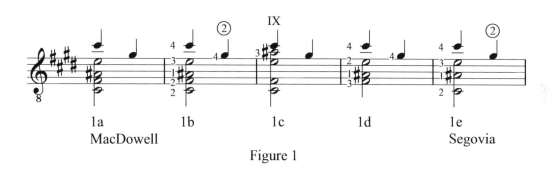

1a
MacDowell

1b

1c

1d

1e
Segovia

Figure 1

The first beat of this measure is a dominant F sharp seventh chord. A first attempt might be, as in Figure 1b, to try to play the whole chord as written. An advantage of this is that all of the chord's tones and its spacing are preserved. One disadvantage of this is simply that it is very difficult to play. Another problem is more complicated and involves the equivalents that were discussed earlier. Different instruments have different affinities for types of chord spacings. A chord formation played on one instrument is not necessarily the equivalent of the same notes played on another instrument. In particular, the piano can produce, more clearly than the guitar, closely spaced intervals—for instance, thirds—in lower registers. This is partly a matter of acoustics; the piano has higher tension, a much longer string length, and greater material density (steel versus nylon) for a given note than the classical guitar. This must be taken into account in making transcriptions of piano music. Equivalent chords on the guitar may require respacing. This is not to say that other factors such as voice leading are less important, but merely that respacing may be a useful solution that helps preserve more of the "aesthetic spirit." In the present transcription the original has also been transposed down a fourth, from A major to E major. Low-pitched chords put an even greater demand on the guitar.

These observations suggest respacing the chord, possibly as in Figure 1c. This preserves but rearranges the whole chord. We have all the notes and it is easier to play. Now another problem arises. The A sharp is high enough that it overlaps the pitch of the next melody note. The G sharp could easily be heard as the resolution of the A sharp. In spacing the harmony higher we risk compromising the independence of the melody. Also, as in the Figure 1b, we have a five-note chord that must be rolled to some degree—no, I haven't grown my right little fingernail yet. This may not be called for musically. Are there other possibilities?

Eliminating notes may help. The C sharp is in both the bass and the melody. We can simply drop the bass note as in Figure 1d. This, in fact, is what Segovia does later in a similar situation. A disadvantage is that the step-wise movement of the bass—to a B in the next measure—is changed. In this piece the middle voices have an almost entirely harmonic function with little regard for voice leading, and so they can be deleted or transposed without jeopardizing any melodic or contrapuntal qualities. However, the bass, as is often the case, is not as amenable to modification.

Figure 1e is Segovia's solution. He has simplified the chord by deleting the F sharp. This note is the root of the harmony and eliminating it should be done only with caution. In this case, the sound does not seem to be adversely affected and the choice solves several other problems: ease of fingering, adequate spacing, and playing the chord without rolling.

This detailed examination of one chord has produced several possibilities as a transcription and illustrates the method of analysis that I recommend. Which alternative do you prefer? Are there other considerations or possible solutions? I will look at a few more examples in somewhat less detail.

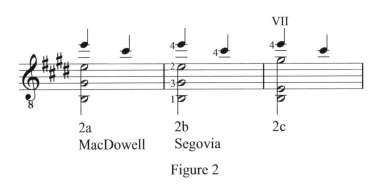

2a
MacDowell

2b
Segovia

2c

Figure 2

In Figure 2b Segovia has directly transferred all notes as written in the original. The only disadvantage that I can see is that it might be too difficult for some players. Overall, the piece is a fairly simple one, perhaps suitable for early intermediate students. For performance, the practical considerations such as a player's ability are no less important than theoretical ones. The respacing shown in Figure 2c may be a useful alternative for some. This type of consideration is not limited to beginning players. It is not necessarily a watering down of the original. There are many examples of truly outstanding players who were apparently unwilling to make pragmatic compromises in transcriptions and, as a result, sacrificed the essence of the music they were trying to perform.

Measure 19 (shown in Figure 3a) seems to lend itself to the same analysis as in Figure 1.

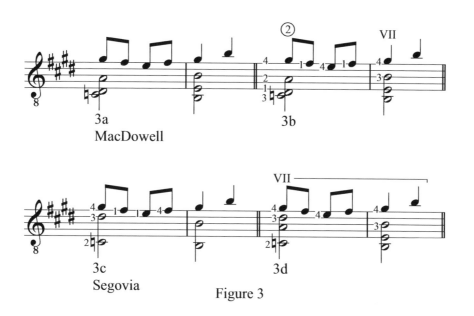

3a
MacDowell

3b

3c
Segovia

3d

Figure 3

Figure 3b is possible, but not being able to hold the D sharp is a disadvantage. Segovia's version is something of a puzzle. He has moved the D sharp up an octave, possibly for clarity, but he has deleted the A. The harmony here is a diminished seventh chord (D sharp-F sharp-A-C natural) with the initial G in the melody acting as a non-chord tone appoggiatura. Leaving out the A greatly affects the perceived harmony by making it sound like a G sharp major (G sharp-B sharp-D sharp). He has also dropped the E from the next measure, changing the harmony from E major to G sharp minor. The result is a G sharp major to G sharp minor progression instead of the original dominant to tonic progression. I have been unable to devise a reason for this, particularly since an easy alternative exists. Perhaps readers will supply some explanations I have overlooked. Figure 3d is another possible transcription of this excerpt. One difference from Segovia's version is playing the melody's E on the third string rather than staying on the second. This is a trade-off between

sustaining the accompaniment and ensuring a consistent tone and articulation in the melody. In this type of situation, Segovia's transcriptions typically favor the melody line.

Starting at measure 24, the melody ascends to its highest point through a series of seventh and ninth chords before returning to the opening theme. The high point is a C sharp at what would be the 21st fret. Segovia has lowered the music by one octave for these five measures. The crux of transcription from piano music is often whether the range of the melody can be handled in a satisfying way. In this piece there is really no possible solution other than lowering this phrase, even though it distorts the whole melodic contour. The transcription either stands or falls, depending on the individual's judgment of the significance of this change.

Two last excerpts are presented for consideration and comment by the readers. How would you solve these? Do you have opinions about the Segovia version? What are the important considerations?

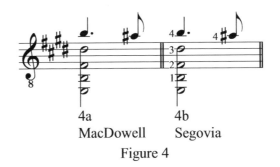

4a
MacDowell

4b
Segovia

Figure 4

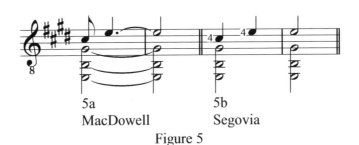

5a
MacDowell

5b
Segovia

Figure 5

Several readers have sent transcriptions for possible publication in *Soundboard* but were too late to be included in this issue. Look for them in future columns. For now I offer a transcription of the *Prelude No. 22* from Alexander Scriabin's *Opus 11*. It was written about the same time as the MacDowell piece in this column, and shares some of the same harmonic vocabulary.

Addendum: Years after writing this column I published a collection of transcriptions of MacDowell's music that included To a Wild Rose. *That transcription was done without reference to the 1996 article; in fact, I had forgotten about the Segovia transcription. So it was with some trepidation that I looked at it to see how my critique of the Segovia version might apply to my own transcription. I was pleased to see that I avoided the shortcomings largely by the choice of key, using D major rather than E major. Although it was not in the original article, I am including it in this collection.*

To a Wild Rose

Transcribed for guitar
by Richard Yates

Op. 51, No. 1

Edward MacDowell
(1861–1908)

With simple tenderness

21

Prelude
Op. 11, No. 22

Transcribed for guitar
by Richard Yates

Alexander Scriabin
(1872–1915)

In Church and Morning Prayer
Peter Tchaikovsky

History provides a vast quantity of works to cull through in the search for music that is suitable for guitar transcription. This can be discouraging unless one can narrow the possibilities for examination. I have often thought this process is like mining for gold: A lot of dirt must be sifted to find the nuggets that make the search worthwhile. We will have better success if we have reliable strategies to follow. One strategy that I have found to be particularly useful is to look at keyboard music written for children.

Since the Baroque period, there has been a tradition of well known composers writing such music. Certainly, J. S. Bach's notebooks for his children are part of this tradition, but other composers have compiled and published similar collections. In this century, Sergei Prokofiev, Claude Debussy, and Heitor Villa-Lobos have written music for children. Robert Schumann's *Album für die Jugend, Opus 68* and Peter Tchaikovsky's *Album for the Young, Opus 39* are good sources. Selections from the second of these two composers are the featured transcriptions in this issue of *Soundboard*.

Music written for children has several characteristics which recommend it as a source for transcriptions. The textures are usually more simple. There is an emphasis on clarity of ideas and simplicity of expression rather than on virtuosity. Pitch range is often smaller than in other keyboard works. However, the smaller scope and lesser complexity of these pieces should not be mistaken for superficiality. The composers have scaled down the size and allowed the qualities of freshness, innocence, and charm to emerge. For guitarists, the music often meets the capabilities of advanced beginner and intermediate players and can provide excellent material for concentrating on particular aspects of technique.

The transcription in this issue is *In Church*, the last piece in Tchaikovsky's *Album for the Young, Op. 39*. This collection contains many pieces of easy to moderate difficulty on the piano; some are considerably more challenging on the guitar. However, *In Church* is the simplest of the lot and many beginners will find it technically easy. Intermediate and even advanced players will find challenges in the subtleties of the phrasing, timbre, articulation, tempo, and dynamics that breathe life into the piece. The simplicity of texture allows a great deal of attention to be directed to these performance aspects, but it also exposes neglect of them.

The transcription itself is relatively straightforward. The key copies the original. All the high chords over the pedal point E had to be dropped an octave and some were reduced from four notes to three, usually by omitting doublings or fifths. The goal was to retain simplicity of execution without sacrificing essential harmony. The only spot that may be hard for players with smaller hands is the G-A#-C chord in measure 31. This has been made as easy as possible by fingering the preceding chord so that all three fingers can be guided by the strings into the stretched position. As you can see, this is one of those pieces that, in transcription, seems almost to have been conceived for the guitar.

Addendum: The original article included a transcription submitted by a Soundboard reader. I am substituting Morning Prayer, another Tchaikovsky piece from the same collection, that works equally well on the guitar and whose transcription involved most of the same considerations.

In Church
Album for the Young, Op. 39

Transcribed for guitar
by Richard Yates

Peter Tchaikovsky
(1840–1893)

Morning Prayer
Album for the Young, Op. 39

Transcribed for guitar
by Richard Yates

Peter Tchaikovsky
(1840–1893)

Sonata, K. 322

Domenico Scarlatti

Difficult do you call it, Sir? I wish it were impossible! —Samuel Johnson

The transcriber looking through keyboard music for suitable material must constantly ask herself a simple question: Is it even possible to play this on the guitar? There can be a wide range of transcribers' willingness to modify the original music, but all too often we are simply confronted with the limitations of the guitar as compared with a keyboard instrument. An objective assessment of these limitations, while dismaying, is also necessary in producing useful musical transcriptions. So how does the guitar measure up as a solo instrument? Well, its pitch range is rather narrow. Its dynamic range is weak. It can only produce four notes simultaneously and has relatively modest contrapuntal agility. There are innumerable combinations of notes that cannot be played because they are either too close together or too far apart, or both. It cannot sustain notes and so can only suggest connected melody. Its variety of timbres is less than the organ or voice. And, a few superhuman players aside, for most of us mortals the guitar can produce notes at only relatively slow tempos. Any one of these limits may eliminate a keyboard piece from serious consideration for transcription to the guitar, but the last one, tempo, is the focus of this article. Transcription inevitably involves modification. The question I will explore is: How is the tempo of a piece affected by transcription to the guitar?

Tempo and Performance

The selection of the tempo of a piece of music is hardly a trivial matter, even when the music is played on the instrument for which it was originally written. It is particularly a problem with music written between 1600 and 1817. Before this span there was a theoretically reliable correlation between time signature and tempo. All tempos were numerically related to a basic, presumably universal, beat—the tactus—which was about 60 to 70 beats per minute. This mensural notation allows us to establish the tempos of modern performances with a high degree of confidence.

In 1817 Beethoven was the first well-known composer to use a recent invention, the metronome, to establish tempos for his music. From this time on, a composer's intentions about tempo could be accurately communicated to the performer. It turned out, however, that even this did not solve the problems. Beethoven himself is said to have radically changed his own previous metronome markings and he once wrote that the metronome was "of no value."

Many guitar transcriptions are from the period with the least agreement about tempo, that is, the Baroque and Classical periods. After 1600 tempo words were increasingly used, while mensural notation declined. Tempo words carried little precision, however. Each theorist of this era seems to have had his own table of tempo words. Not only do these tables contradict each other as to what speeds to attach to particular words, sometimes they even disagree as to the order of quickness, that is, whether allegro is faster or slower than allegretto, etc. Compounding the problem were the overlapping definitions of tempo words. Some were descriptions of moods, as in allegro (cheerful). Others described speed, as in lento (slow). Over time some mood words came to have speed meanings, but others did not. The result is considerable uncertainty.

Underlying most of the debates about tempos was another concept that was thought to bring some coherence to it all—the tempo giusto—but even this term brings confusion in that it is sometimes used to mean "strict tempo." It is the other meaning to which I refer: Tempo giusto means the "right tempo." The idea was that each piece of music has an implicit and discoverable correct tempo. Leopold Mozart said that inferring the correct tempo from the score "infallibly shows the true quality of a musician." The implication was that the tempo words could get you to the right neighborhood and then your refined sense of the tempo giusto could take over for the fine tuning, so to speak.

I will show you some hard evidence that bears on this question a little further on, but we must first recognize that the foregoing has shed little light on the central question about tempo and transcription. The question might be reworded at this point: Does the tempo giusto of a piece of music change when it is played on a different instrument? In fact, I have found in music literature no direct reference to this issue at all. The only remaining avenues for investigation are unfettered, but informed, speculation and observation of the actual performance practice of the best players.

Tempo and Transcription

There are several qualities of the guitar itself that may affect tempos. Certainly, as an instrument that cannot sustain tones, the guitar has definite lower limits of reasonable tempo in slow pieces. Bowed string instruments, organ or voice can shape a coherent line using tempos that would completely fragment the melody on the guitar, or the piano. Although—as Ralph Kirkpatrick wrote about nonsustaining instruments—"It is not sound but mental expectation that produces musical continuity," there are still real, practical limits to this principle.

What of the other end of the spectrum? It seems that there are reasons for a lower tempo giusto on the guitar. First, there is the often overlooked fact that the guitar is a low pitched instrument. Since guitar music is usually written with an octave transposition—or with a small "8" at the bottom of the clef—it is easy to forget that the E on the first string twelfth fret is only the top space on a regular treble staff, and the open sixth string is below the bottom of a staff with a bass clef. The overall pitch of an instrument has implications for tempo. Lower pitches are slower to speak. Larger forces and movements are required to set the string in motion, and the acoustic events that follow the plucking of the string take longer to play out. As a result, rapid notes have less clarity than they would if pitched higher. In addition, the guitar's shorter string lengths, compared to, say, the harpsichord, mean lower tensions and less clarity.

A more subtle point relates to difficulty. Technically, the guitar presents monumental obstacles to speed compared to a keyboard instrument. Each note played on the guitar usually requires two fingers. Successive notes require extremely precise coordination of fingers on both hands. The point is not just that a guitar cannot be played as fast as a keyboard, it is that the perceived difficulty, including speed and complexity, is part of the total experience of the listener. To quote Kirkpatrick again, "Perhaps the very opposition with which the artist is confronted by the tools and materials of his medium is a stimulant necessary in some measure to the intensity and concentration of his communication through domination of that medium." Most guitar music played on the piano sounds thin—it presents little opposition, in Kirkpatrick's words—and it is natural ("giusto") to play it faster. Conversely, the guitar gives us more opposition, and hence, slower tempos may fit better.

Earlier in this article I made unflattering

comparisons of the guitar's capabilities, and of course only told half the story. While on each of the dimensions I listed (pitch range, dynamics, complexity, etc.) the guitar is far surpassed by other instruments, it may be that no other instrument has as great a variety of these dimensions within which one can create artistic nuances. It may be the most versatile of instruments, in that it can produce distinctions in more ways. The violin is sadly lacking in contrapuntal ability, the harpsichord cannot vary loudness at all, and the piano always has the same timbre. The guitar can do these things and more, simultaneously. Well played guitar music presents the listener with a wealth of subtle variations and nuances of sound. This is a lot of information to process. Perhaps the tempo giusto depends on the rate of information. If this is so, then slower tempos are necessary in performing guitar transcriptions. Of course, this assumes that the player is doing something artistic with all of the instrument's potential. Sadly, we have all heard fast players that were giving us only rapid notes. The British guitarist Stephen Kenyon wrote on this point, "We are used to hearing a certain amount of information—hopefully what the player intended—and if they play too fast sometimes we do not recognize that and then subconsciously we think 'this player's boring.' This certainly happens with some very fast players I can think of. They proudly play perhaps Bach or Paganini at exactly the tempi of the fiddlers, but after the gasps of astonishment have subsided—assuming they do—they are often, I find, boring."

Sources of Information

The foregoing discussion is mostly speculation. I felt a need to find some hard data in hopes that it would provide a firmer foundation to my theorizing. Leopold Mozart's advice seemed a logical way to pursue the question. I decided to find as many examples as I could of music played on both the guitar and keyboard to see how tempos varied with the instrument and the performer. To cut down the size of the search I focused on two composers: Domenico Scarlatti and Enrique Granados. Both composers wrote keyboard music that has been transcribed and recorded many times, and so provided lots of data points from which to observe patterns and draw conclusions. I later narrowed the search further when I found out which particular pieces had been recorded the most. While there were a few recordings in my own collection and at the local library that I could actually listen to and measure with the infamous metronome, I needed more information. How I obtained this was a fascinating experience that I hope will be a useful digression for readers. Those of you who are already connected to the Internet may find a few new resources mentioned here; those who have yet to connect may find that there are good reasons to do so.

Without access to many actual recordings, I resorted to the next best source of information about tempo—the timings that were listed for the music. The samples that I could listen to confirmed that the overall timings of pieces gave a reliable measure for comparing average tempo. The advantage of using this measure was that it gave me access to many recordings through library catalogs and other people's collections. In fact, all the data that I will describe was collected from my home computer. I have listed some sites at the end of this article.

On the Internet I was able to get into the online catalog for a network of 13 college and university libraries in Oregon and Washington (ORBIS). In one afternoon I also accessed the entire University of California catalog (MELVYL), the New York Public Library, and the United States Library of Congress. All of these electronic catalogs allow detailed, automated searches. I simply had to type in what I was looking for—for example, audio recordings of *Sonata K. 322* by Domenico Scarlatti. Almost instantly I could scan all of the catalog entries that applied. Although only about 20 percent of the catalog listings included the timings of individual pieces, I could quickly find a great deal of relevant information in a short time that I could not have collected at all without the Internet.

A second source of information was an e-mail discussion group devoted to the topic of classical guitar. Group members contributed both opinions and data from their collections. Known as the Classical Guitar Mailing List (CGML), this is a group of several hundred people from all over the world with a common love of the guitar who engage in lively and interesting discussions through e-mail. Each message is automatically sent to all members of the group or "list" and an average day includes about 30 messages. The exchange of ideas from players—both amateur and professional—writers, luthiers, teachers, and students is stimulating, educational and a useful source of information, as in the present example. The CGML is deftly and diplomatically administered by the Portland, Oregon, guitarist and teacher, John Philip Dimick.

Evidence from Performances

For this article I have collected the timings for two pieces. They are well known works that have been frequently recorded. The first is the *Harpsichord Sonata in E Major, K. 380* by Domenico Scarlatti. The second is the *Intermezzo* from *Goyescas* by Enrique Granados. The performance data for these two pieces is typical of all that I collected. The following tables list the performer, the instrument(s), and the timings.

Harpsichord Sonata in E Major, K. 380, Domenico Scarlatti

Anthony Newman	harpsichord	4:25
Wanda Landowska	harpsichord	4:35
Trevor Pinnock	harpsichord	4:45
Ida Presti and Alexandre Lagoya	guitar duo	4:47
Ivo Pogorelich	piano	4:59
Ida Presti and Alexandre Lagoya	guitar duo	5:03
Eliot Fisk	guitar	5:04
John Sankey	MIDI harpsichord	5:04
Dinu Lapatti	piano	5:12
John Williams	guitar	5:16
Eliot Fisk (1985)	guitar	5:16
Manuel Barrueco	guitar	5:20
Dinu Lapatti	piano	5:26
Groniger Duo	guitar duo	5:26
Kaare Norge	guitar	5:35
John Browning	harpsichord	5:42
Mikhail Pletnev	harpsichord	5:44
Edoardo Catemario	guitar	5:47
Igor Kipnis	harpsichord	5:56
Rafael Puyana	harpsichord	6:00
Christain Zacharias	piano	6:04
Vladimir Horowitz	piano	6:20

Meiko Miyazawa	piano	6:21
Vladimir Horowitz (1968)	piano	6:22
Carlos Barbosa-Lima	guitar	6:22
Luciano Sgrizzi	harpsichord	6:40

The first table shows harpsichords as the quickest, but Presti and LaGoya and then Eliot Fisk are very close. Other eminent harpsichordists are further back. Overall, there seems to be very little correlation between tempo and instrument.

Intermezzo from *Goyescas,* Enrique Granados

Sergio and Eduardo Abreu	guitar duo	4:03
Arthur Fiedler	Boston Pops	4:21
Casals and Mednikoff	cello and piano	4:28
John Williams and Julian Bream	guitar duo	4:45
Trio Sonata	flute, oboe and guitar	4:53
Paul Brody and George Brough	saxophone and piano	5:05
Raphael Frühbeck de Burgos	New Philharmonia	5:16
United States Marine Band	military band	5:23
Marek Jerie and Konrad Ragossnig	cello and guitar	5:25
Fritz Reiner	Chicago Symphony	5:31

The second table has a wide, and sometimes improbable, array of instruments, but again, there is no correlation with tempo that I can see. Guitars and orchestras span the whole range of tempos at which the *Intermezzo* has been recorded. The objective evidence seems to show that there is not a correlation between instrument and tempo.

But can we also conclude that the mystical tempo giusto is maintained as a piece of music is transferred from instrument to instrument? Not at all! And this is what I find most striking about the data. There is no evidence whatsoever for an implicit tempo in this music. There is a tremendous range, and smooth distribution, of tempos chosen for the same music by skilled and highly regarded performers. The slowest performances of the Scarlatti sonata are at 70 beats per minute; the fastest is more than 105 beats, a full 50 percent increase.

My conclusion from all this is that as transcribers and performers, we can, with ample justification, ignore speed contests and comparisons, and instead confidently select the music for which we have an affinity and fill the silence with the endlessly varied sound that can be uniquely produced by our guitars and our selves.

Featured Transcription

The transcription I selected for this issue is one I made in the course of my research for this article. It is one of Scarlatti's most familiar harpsichord sonatas, and one that has often been recorded on the classical guitar. In my search I found eight guitar and five piano recordings; oddly enough, there were no harpsichord recordings. I thought it would be a good piece for readers to try out with the discussion about tempo in mind.

While Scarlatti is best known for his more than 500 harpsichord sonatas, it is important to remember that his father and teacher, Alessandro Scarlatti, was a prolific opera composer, and Domenico himself produced mostly operas until rather late in life. The sonatas bear all the signs of his early experience. They are, above all, theatrical. Phrases call and answer each other, voices join in duets, hunting horns sound and horses gallop, bulls charge and thunder crashes, all in contrasting episodes highly evocative of dramatic scenes. There is tremendous opportunity here for the broad use of tonal contrasts and agogic accents. This music is the strongest argument I know to refute the stereotype of Baroque music as mechanical and cerebral.

The *Sonata in A Major, K. 322* is marked "Allegro," which, as we have already seen, means different things to different people. Narciso Yepes blazed through it at 111 beats per minute. John Williams, Carlos Barbosa-Lima, Rachel Gauk, and Eliot Fisk were all clocked at about 100, Andrés Segovia came in at 90, and a pianist, Andras Schiff, played it at a leisurely 77 beats per minute. My suggestion is that you play it no faster and no slower than that which makes perfect sense to you.

Two final notes: The Longo number for this sonata is L. 483, but I have seen two references to it—one on a John Williams album cover—as L. 485. Also, there is a marvelous website listed in the references (below) that has a huge number of downloadable MIDI files. Included are all of the Scarlatti sonatas performed by the harpsichordist John Sankey. These and other similar sites are a magnificent resource for transcribers who are listening for music that may be suitable for the guitar.

As always, I look forward to hearing readers' reactions, comments, and suggestions.

References and Suggested Browsing

Classical MIDI Archives, www.prs.net/midi.html

Cyr, Mary (1992). *Performing Baroque Music*, Amadeus Press, Portland, Oregon.

Donington, Robert (1982). *Baroque Music: Style and Performance*, W. W. Norton, New York

Kirkpatrick, Ralph (1984). *Interpreting Bach's Well-Tempered Clavier*, Yale University Press, New Haven.

University of California Libraries, www.melvyl.ucop.edu

U.S. Library of Congress, www.loc.gov

Sonata
K. 322

Transcribed for guitar
by Richard Yates

Domenico Scarlatti
(1683–1757)

Prélude á Jeanne Leleu

Maurice Ravel

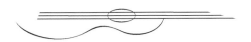

The place was Paris, France; the date, April 20, 1910; the event, the inaugural concert of the Société Musicale Indépendente. The music was the world premier of piano duets by the foremost composer of the day, Maurice Ravel. In spite of the enormous pressure on the players, the composer was greatly pleased by the performance. He wrote to one of the pianists,

"Mademoiselle, when you are a great virtuosa and I either an old fogey, covered with honors, or else completely forgotten, you will perhaps have pleasant memories of having given an artist the very rare joy of hearing a work of his, one of a rather special nature, interpreted exactly as it should be. Thank you a thousand times for your child-like and sensitive performance...."

The pianist who received this lavish praise? Jeanne Leleu, age seven!

Mlle. Leleu was apparently not a child prodigy, but she did later have a career as a concert pianist. Three years after this recital, Ravel wrote a short prelude that he dedicated to her and which is the featured transcription of this installment of *The Transcriber's Art*. It is a charming miniature, rarely heard, and I believe not previously transcribed for guitar. It is guitar-sized for the most part, although the range is a bit wider than we guitarists are comfortable with—more on this problem soon. Ravel's comments on the music for Mlle. Leleu's recital might well have been made about the *Prélude*, "My intention of awakening the poetry of childhood in these pieces naturally led me to simplify my style and thin out my writing."

Impressionism

Although its roots were earlier, impressionism in music is usually first associated with Claude Debussy. The term was originally used to describe painting techniques that employed a deliberate avoidance of sharp outlines. The transfer of the term to music is often metaphorical and, well, "impressionistic," but implies a lack of definite structural form and avoidance of clear tonal centers. There is an abundance of unresolved dissonances, harmonies with added notes, parallel chords, and whole tone scales.

In attempting transcriptions of impressionistic music to the guitar we find characteristics that ease the task, but also those that make it more difficult. The harmonic language includes chords with many different notes. The usual solution to large chords—deleting duplicate notes—often does not apply and we are left with more difficult decisions. Even if there is a relatively satisfying solution that retains the essential notes, the smaller chord will still give sharper "edges" to what originally was more "blurred." Ironically, deleting nonharmonic or dissonant notes from a large chord may actually draw more attention to those that remain and make the sonority sound more dissonant. On the other hand, impressionistic harmonies, and even melodies, can often be altered without substantially changing the overall sonority. There can be many equivalent ways to achieve the same impression. To the extent that transcription involves recomposition based on what is perceived to be the original intention of the composer, impressionistic music allows us more freedom than, say, a Baroque fugue. Lest this be considered a cavalier lack of appreciation of the subtleties of impressionistic music, consider the parallel case with painting. Altering specific elements of a highly realistic painting would be immediately obvious and a clear violation of the painter's intent. With an impressionistic painting there could be many elements modified without noticeable effect. An assumption of impressionism is that appearances do change as circumstances, such as the light, change. It seems reasonable to similarly assume that sound changes as circumstances, such as the instrument, change. The details discussed below may help clarify these ideas.

Prélude á Mademoiselle Jeanne Leleu

While most of the transcription of the *Prélude* was straightforward—we can be thankful that Ravel did thin out his writing—there are several points that may be of interest to readers.

The first concerns the bass lines in measures 4, 6, and 8 of the transcription. Play through them if you would, please. Did you notice anything amiss? My hope is that you did not, of course, but the facts are that I changed some notes outright in these bass lines. Now, transcribers change notes all the time. Usually, however, they move them up and down octaves, add notes in an established harmony, and certainly delete lots of them. But here I have blatantly changed a few. The original lines looked like this (transposed up a fifth to match the guitar version).

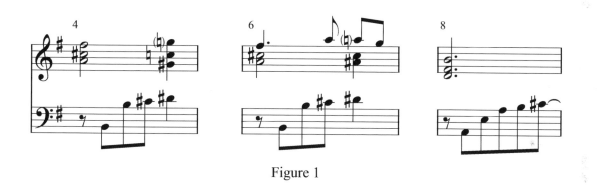

Figure 1

The problem is that common one—the guitar's range is too narrow. If this were a Mozart piano sonata, we might try the octave transposition trick, but that would miss the point. The essential feature of this bass is its shape more than its specific pitches. Here, the way to preserve the shape is to change the pitches, hence my solution. Note also that the result in measures 4 and 6 is a short whole tone scale, one of the characteristic features of this music. Measure 8 presents a slightly different problem as there is no lower note that can be substituted for the low A. The solution, as you can see, is to turn the eighth rest into a quarter rest and simply leave out the A. Here the shape of the line is more important than the rhythm. Ravel has even told us this at the head of the piece: "d'un rhythme libre" (with a free rhythm). So, the shape has been saved and the rhythm sacrificed.

Another interesting spot is at measure 12, but first some background. The blurring of structure and outlines in impressionistic piano music often takes advantage of the damper pedal. When it is pressed, notes continue to sound even after the key is released. There is then an overlapping of harmonies that blends and disguises the progressions. The only score of this piece that I have found indicates that the damper pedal is to be pressed at the beginning of measure 2, and there is no indication to release it until measure

22! Although it is possible that this is a typographical error—please let me know if you have any authoritative information on this—it is also consistent with an impressionistic approach. Transcription should try to find equivalents for this on the guitar, for example, using cross-string scales where possible and playing scales in such a way as to allow subsequent tones to overlap. At the least, attempts should be made to preserve the written length of notes.

Now, look at measure 12 and notice the left-hand fingering. Contrary to what I have just said, the fingering does not allow the half notes C and E to sustain for their full value; they appear to have been abruptly shortened by half. Time for another digression (I promise we really will get to the point soon).

Each note sounded on an instrument is actually a combination of many different pitches called harmonics or overtones. We mainly hear the lowest of these, called the fundamental, but there are also present, in ascending order, the next octave above the fundamental, the perfect fifth above that, then the perfect fourth, major third, minor third, and so on. The relative strengths of these partials largely account for the differences in tone color between instruments.

We take advantage of these overtones when we play natural or artificial harmonics on the guitar. When we do this, we stop (damp) the fundamental and lower overtones from sounding and allow the upper ones to ring through. This phenomenon of vibrating strings also shows itself in another way. A string that is not plucked, but is in the presence of sound (usually from another string), will vibrate if it has overtones that match the pitch coming from the string that has been plucked. This is called sympathetic vibration. Try this experiment. Put your second finger on the first string, fifth fret. Pluck the string strongly, being careful not to touch any other strings with your left- or right-hand

fingers. Silence the string immediately after you have plucked it, again without touching any other strings. Listen closely. You will hear that A note continuing after you silence the first string. Do the experiment again, but this time lightly rest the first finger of your left hand across the strings as if holding a barré on the fourth fret, but only to muffle these strings. The A note stops dead this time. With a little more experimentation you will find that the fifth string carries on the high A (its third harmonic) as does the fourth string (its second harmonic).

Sympathetic vibration can be enlisted as the damper pedal of the guitar as I have done in measure 12. Pluck the three-string chord that starts the measure. Be sure to only barré the top three strings. Silence the three strings immediately. You will find that the E note has been picked up sympathetically by the fifth string (its second harmonic) and by the sixth string (its third harmonic). This sympathetic E covers the shift in position as you move on to the second beat of the measure.

My rather long-winded explanation of this fingering technique may seem out of proportion to the effect that it produces, but as you examine printed editions and make your own decisions about fingerings you will find that it can often be quite helpful. Attention to this phenomenon will also sharpen your ear for other details of sound that are easy to overlook but which contribute substantially to the musical effect that you produce.

I hope that you enjoy the *Prélude*, and as you play you might try to imagine yourself in as prestigious and historic a moment as Mlle. Leleu was and live up to the praise she received from the composer.

Prélude
á Mademoiselle Jeanne Leleu

Transcribed for guitar
by Richard Yates

Maurice Ravel (1913)

Assez lent et très expressif (d'un rythme libre)

ralenti   *au mouvt.*

ralenti   *decresc.*   **pp** *très lent*

Waltz, Op. 39, No. 11

Johannes Brahms

I don't think necessity is the mother of invention—invention arises directly from ... laziness. To save oneself trouble. —Agatha Christie (1890–1976)

Transcribing music, as it involves moving a unified artistic construction from one medium to another, can be well-defined in many of its technical aspects, but trying to explain the subtleties often forces people to resort to metaphors. Andrés Segovia compared it to translating a poem from one language to another. I have often thought of transcription as mining tons of ore to find a few gems to cut and polish for the delight of others. Another metaphor that has recently come to mind is that of a wilderness guide. Having discovered a fabulous destination, the guide must then find the most expeditious route and cut a trail to ease the passage. After all, if his clients have to work too hard on the trek, they will have little inclination or opportunity to absorb the beauty of the territory along the way. And when they, in turn, through musical performance, take an audience on the journey, the art in the music will be less encumbered by the task of producing it. And who would deny that the task of producing music on the guitar can be an arduous one?

Guide Fingers

Now, I must confess that, faced with the guitar's idiosyncrasies, laziness is, and must be, one of my primary motivators when making a transcription. Unfortunately, at times I lose sight of laziness as a guiding principle and I am overcome with grandiose delusions about my technical abilities, only to be abruptly brought to my senses with the realization that my skills are not adequate to play a transcription that I have made. I then scramble to find ways to ease the difficulties: drop a note here, cross out a tie there, shift a bar down an octave. But these all change the original music—sometimes more than is judicious. In the search for efficient means of finding and sustaining notes, the trick that often comes to my rescue—a bridge across an unfordable stream if you will—is the topic of this article: the guide finger.

There are many individual differences that affect fingerings; hand size, shape, strength and flexibility vary so much that there can be no universally correct fingering, and of course I have not even mentioned the aesthetic and musical factors that influence fingering choices. However, there are a small number of basic principles that universally apply. Certainly, fingerings that embody efficient motions are to be preferred, as are those that promote security and accuracy of left-hand shifts. These latter values urge the thoughtful use of guide fingers. Most guitarists are familiar with this concept: A guide finger is a left-hand finger that can slide along a string when there is a shift from one position to another. The guide finger can then easily find its correct position and, in addition, provide kinesthetic reference around which the other fingers can arrange themselves. While this is covered early in guitar instruction, guide fingers come in a variety of forms, some of which are not so obvious and, judging from editions that I have seen, not recognized by some good players.

I selected this issue's featured transcription because of the relatively large number and type of guide fingers that it includes. I don't see any value in making an exhaustive inventory of the guide fingers used in this piece—I will leave it to the reader to find all 27 of them—but I hope that, by looking at a few examples, players may be more likely to recognize similar situations and even discover new ones. If you can do so, then you will lighten the load you take on in performance or that you give to other players in transcriptions you make.

Examples in the Score

The shift from measure 14 to measure 15 uses a guide finger in its basic form. Please note that I use the common convention of a short dash in front of a left-hand fingering number to show that the finger arrived at that place as a guide finger. The 4 finger holds the D sharp and then slides up the second string to the F sharp. Here the guide finger serves the musical choice of keeping the melody on one string. This maintains evenness of tone and, at the discretion of the player, permits a slight glissando up to, and then vibrato on, the dissonant note. My guess is that most players would use the guide finger so naturally here that it would feel awkward not to. But where are the less obvious examples I have claimed?

The fingering of the second beat of measure six would be most naturally, and naively, to use the 2 finger on the G and the 3 finger on the

E. But this means that in the shift to the third beat, the 1, 2 and 3 fingers must all move simultaneously to different strings and different frets. Many players can do this with little trouble, but surely the fingering I have suggested in the score makes the shift more reliable. In anticipation of the shift, the 3 finger is used for the G—a slightly more unusual choice—so that it can remain on the second string on beat three and the 1 and 2 fingers can more easily find their proper places.

There is a more obscure, perhaps even puzzling, use of a guide finger from measure three to measure four. The note B starting at measure four is fingered by the 3 finger and is apparently a guide finger, but the 3 finger is not used at all in the preceding measure. What is going on here? Well, my suggestion is that the 3 finger be placed on the third string A note on the last beat of measure three even though it is not a sounded note. This three-finger configuration of an A minor chord is one of the most natural and well-ingrained for all guitarists. It therefore costs nothing but a little forethought to make the shift to measure four slightly more secure. Over the course of an entire piece it is important to accumulate advantages such as this, however small they may be. Skeptical and observant readers may ask: Why use the 3 finger for the B at all? The answer is that it is then used as yet another version of the guide finger—one that does not move at all. The fingering starting at measure five needs very accurate placement to sustain the G and to execute the grace note well. Arranging—way back in measure three—to have the 3 finger already on the correct string helps ease this obstacle. A similar, but slightly different situation arises in measure 24 where a guide finger is set up well in advance. Often these cases are discovered by working backward in assigning fingerings. When you have a spot that is troublesome and can be fingered only one way, look to see if there are non-standard fingerings on the previous beat that will facilitate the shift, and then see how you can arrive at those. You may find that the solution to a tough spot comes by preparing several measures earlier. If you are blazing a trail for others to follow you want to consider all of the possibilities and so save others the trouble.

Brahms' *Waltz, Op. 39, No. 11*

I have found very few of Brahms' piano pieces that work in transcription. He tended to use the whole keyboard in long waves that sound feeble when broken into narrowly pitched chunks to fit the guitar's range. However, as with nearly all of the best composers, he also understood the value of smaller scale pieces that communicate a sentiment concisely and briefly. The featured transcription is one of these. When you are not picking your way through the many guide fingers, you will find it to be a sweet and rhythmic dance with a few gentle harmonic surprises.

Waltz

Op. 39, No. 11

Transcribed for guitar
by Richard Yates

Johannes Brahms
(1833–1897)

This page has been left blank to avoid awkward page turns.

Prelude XXI

The Well-Tempered Clavier, Book I

Johann Sebastian Bach

There seems to be no limit to the demand for classical guitar transcriptions of the music of Johann Sebastian Bach. A perusal of music catalogs, recital programs, and websites reveals our nearly insatiable appetite for such editions, and a primary focus of our desires has always been the preludes and fugues from that monument of musical history, *The Well-Tempered Clavier* (WTC). And yet, with the hunger for the music comes a proportional challenge to the transcriber.

We tend to regard the WTC with a reverence that makes us reluctant to dare make the modifications that are inevitable in transcriptions. We can be caught between attraction to the music and fear that altering it would somehow be sacrilegious. Well, maybe we just need to get over that and accept the reality that all transcriptions change the original. Our transcriptions can stand or fall on their own merits. The solidity with which Bach's music is carved into history could, instead, give us more freedom to attempt daring and idiosyncratic transcriptions, secure in the knowledge that there is no risk our altered versions might displace the original. Yet, with this freedom also comes a responsibility to approach Bach transcriptions with a high degree of attention to detail and to carefully weigh decisions that will clearly be seen as our own personal creative elements. An excellent articulation of this approach is found in *J. S. Bach: Six Unaccompanied Cello Suites Arranged for Guitar*, transcribed by Stanley Yates (Mel Bay Publications, 1998).

Having allayed our anxiety about the Transcription Police, we are confronted with the next obstacle. There is a practical problem: Bach's music is so artfully constructed that it includes little excess that can be pared away to reveal the essential elements to preserve in transcription. It often all seems to be essential. This is especially problematic with his keyboard music, where some reduction is almost always necessary to make it playable. Personally, I have found no Bach keyboard fugues that I can, with a clear conscience, play on the guitar, and this issue must be kept in mind as we look closer at the WTC.

The Well-Tempered Clavier

The WTC is arranged as 48 pairs of preludes and fugues written in all the major and minor keys. The pairs are apparently intended to be, and commonly are, played together. Much has been written about the construction of these pairs. Some have thematic connections—although occasionally the connection seems to be solely in the minds of musicologists—while others were assembled by joining compositions that Bach had previously written in other keys and for other purposes. The original pairing of a prelude with a fugue need not be of concern to us in transcribing a prelude, if it can stand alone as a musically satisfying whole. In the featured transcription, this issue is in some doubt and so we will turn to the score to investigate further.

Prelude XXI

Prelude XXI from the first book of *The Well-Tempered Clavier* has the character of a freely improvised fantasia or toccata. Sweeping scales alternate with arpeggiated sequences and block chords. There is a strong similarity to lute suite preludes of the time, which had the musical task of setting the key and the practical purpose of checking the instrument's tuning and limbering the fingers. And a guitarist had better be quite limber to play this at the tempo that pianists often do. Perhaps pianists are misled by the notation in thirty-second notes. Or having so little that they can do with individual notes, compared to guitarists, they are obligated to squeeze as many as they can into a short period of time to hide this shortcoming of their instrument. (I hope that regular readers will forgive this one last, brief rant on the topic). Needless to say, a presentation that is graceful, rhythmic, and quick—but not blindingly fast—can be very effective. One pianist's recording is at a tempo of about 140 quarter notes per minute, but a tempo as sedate as 90 will work. This is not to say that you shouldn't turn on the after-burners if you want to, only that it is not necessary. Actually, it is fun to play it fast, and in fingering the piece I have given a high priority to facilitating speed by using helpful slurs and an occasional thumb in the scales, and by avoiding awkward string crossings, stretches and long position shifts.

The Transcription

A first glance at the keyboard score shows a frightening and unrelenting series of thirty-second notes straight through the first page. To lessen the intimidation factor, conserve ink, and allow a more agreeable page layout, I have doubled all of the note values and halved the measures. In this case it has no effect on the actual performance information conveyed by the score.

Having cleared some space to see better, a second look at the score immediately shows the actual obstacles, and perhaps the reason guitarists have bypassed this piece. There are long sweeping scales through more octaves than we have available. In many poor transcriptions, a scale run that suddenly jumps an octave and then continues can be jarring and is identified at once as a display of the limitations of the instrument and the transcriber's imagination. The failure can be painfully obvious. But let's not let this risk daunt us; although some scales must be chopped up, we still have viable choices about where jumps occur.

The first task is to choose a key that minimizes the number of such problems. Here, transposing to A major from the original B flat works well, as it places the melody so it makes use of the full range of the guitar up to that high B natural. We can find some reassurance in the fact that we will have only scale notes there and no chords. Yet, even with this key choice there are two places where a cut, transposed and spliced scale line cannot be avoided. The first is in measure 16. In the original the second note, A, is a third lower than the C that starts the measure. The octave transposition of the A and the following notes is quite acceptable for a couple of reasons. The leap upwards becomes only a sixth, not a seventh. Also, and more persuasive, the scalar movement ending measure 15 has the A note as its apparent destination. In the transcription, the first half of measure 16 now serves as a means of reaching that note on the second beat of the measure. The result is a musically sensible one. Although I have had to move the line up an octave, the contour of the key notes is still a downward one. Reinforcing this alteration is the similarity of the gesture to that in the first half of measure 20. The second instance of an octave transposition within a scale is in measure 24. Here the leap upward is a seventh, but a key point is that it is a minor seventh, not a major one. What's the difference? Well, the minor seventh leap and following notes outline a dominant seventh harmony that will then resolve to an implied F sharp major and then to the solid downbeat in measure 25 on the temporary tonic of B minor: a II7-V-I cadence. In this context, the notes C sharp and B natural are not just adjacent scale tones rudely separated. They are harmonically essential, and so the leap actually helps define the harmonic progression. My comments about the overall contour of the line at measure 16 also apply here. At a brisk tempo the C sharp just before the leap is heard as resolving naturally to the B in measure 25. So both the melodic and the harmonic essentials are maintained in the transcription, in spite of the changes.

Most of the other changes that were necessary in making the transcription are unremarkable, such as the revoicing of the block chords to make them guitar-friendly. I would also mention that I have added editorial accent marks (>), as in measure 22. The shape of the line and the free, improvisatory nature of the piece prompted these additions to help clarify the rhythm as I understand it.

The one defect that I see in this transcription is not in the music, but in the fact that nothing follows it. It is truly a prelude in the introductory sense but, sadly, not complemented by a fugue. If you know of one that could be paired with it and that works on the guitar in A major, please let me know.

Addendum: It was interesting to see that when writing this article I did not know, of course, that I would later find a Bach fugue from the WTC that worked well on the guitar. Happily, that transcription seems to be a logical extension of my evolution as a transcriber. You can find the transcription and article later in this book. It was completely fortuitous that the key of that fugue, D major, does make it well-suited for pairing with Prelude XXI. *Although they are not in the same key—unlike all the pairs in the* WTC—*when played before the fugue, the prelude acts as an extended dominant chord satisfyingly resolved by the entrance of the fugue theme. For a radical modification of the prelude, change the last note from A natural to G natural to give it a true dominant seventh function—and a bit easier reach, too!*

Prelude XXI
Well Tempered Clavier, Book 1

Transcribed for guitar
by Richard Yates

J. S. Bach
(1685–1750)

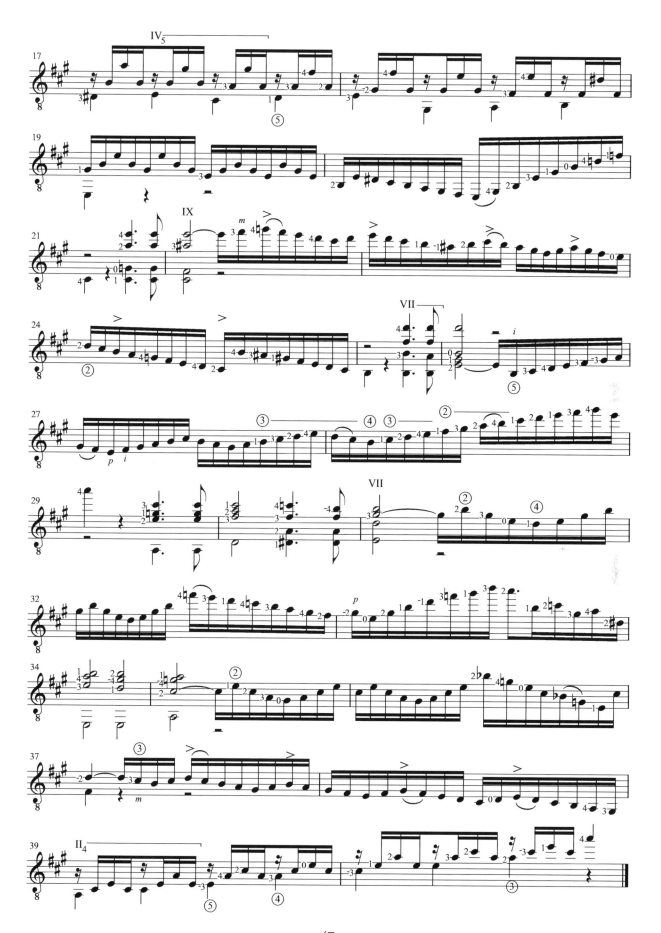

47

This page has been left blank to avoid awkward page turns.

Three Short Pieces

Girolamo Kapsberger

It is near the height of the Renaissance in Italy, 1611, where there is an unprecedented concentration of musical genius. Giovanni Gabrieli is the organist at St. Mark's cathedral in Venice—where he teaches Heinrich Schutz—while Girolamo Frescobaldi holds the same position in Rome. Carlo Gesualdo is writing madrigals with astonishing harmonies in Naples, and Claudio Monteverdi's landmark opera, *Orfeo*, has recently been produced. Fretted instruments have reached a peak of popularity, and although it has been a couple decades since the death of Vincenzo Galilei, there is a new generation of lutenist/composers on the scene, including Alesssandro Piccinini and Simone Molinaro. So, who was the best known and most widely respected lute performer and composer in this historic hotbed of fretboard creativity? Surprisingly, it was someone whose name most guitarists have never heard: Johann Hieronymus Kapsberger, also known by his Italianized first names, Giovanni Girolamo. Why his place in the musical pantheon has declined in the last 400 years is an interesting story.

Kapsberger was born of German parents in Venice around 1580. By his early 20s he had developed a powerful technique and published the first-ever book of solo theorbo music. He was soon employed by the papal family in Rome, where he stayed for most of his career. His musical output includes, in addition to lute and theorbo music, songs, operas, and motets. He was renowned as both performer and composer but the degree of his virtuosity was apparently matched by his ego and arrogance. A friend and

musical theorist who had earlier praised him, was later sharply disparaging. Although this attack apparently had little effect on Kapsberger's popularity at the time, it is the spin that became incorporated into the music history books and was repeated through the years until the last century. One lesson transcribers can take from this is to be cautious in accepting conventional wisdom about the worth of a composer's music. There may be gold where many say there is only dross.

The Music

For this issue's featured transcriptions I have selected three pieces from Kapsberger's known works. Although six have been lost, today we have four books of his music for both lute and chitarrone. This latter instrument, also known as the theorbo, was similar to the lute but had a greatly extended neck to accommodate unstopped bass strings that were about twice the length of the stopped courses—some instruments approached two meters in length. By 1600, shortly before Kapsberger was approaching his decades of fame, the chitarrone had become a favorite instrument in Italy for accompanying singers. Although its most common use was accompaniment, there is a sizeable body of solo music written for it. The earliest and highest quality was written by Kapsberger.

I have assembled a short suite from a toccata, originally for chitarrone, followed by a gagliarda and a corrente, originally for lute. Remember that it was only a couple of decades later that the Baroque suite first appeared from Froberger; it seems likely that collections such as Kapsberger's presage that development. His books are arranged so that pieces of the same type appear together. I think it is no coincidence that in his lute book of 1611 the toccatas, a free form later to become the prelude, are followed by the gagliardas, and then the correntes—a similar order as in a suite. It may be that the intention was for the player to select from each of these types to construct an informal suite as I have done here. As with a suite, my purpose is to show you a variety of pieces with a similar scope by one composer.

On the Edge

As you play the transcriptions you may find them to be interesting from another historical perspective. Kapsberger's compositions delicately balance Renaissance and Baroque styles. He embodied the Early Baroque spirit of adventure and exploration, and the *Toccata* here certainly seems straight Baroque—it could easily be passed off as something written by Sylvius Leopold Weiss or even J. S. Bach. Yet the *Gagliarda* is pure Renaissance, while the *Corrente* has elements of both. Playing through many Kapsberger pieces gives one a clear vision into the events of this remarkable period in the history of music. It was a time when the musical paradigm was in flux, a time of experimentation. Some of Kapsberger's experiments strain and fall short of being convincing, but others succeed wonderfully.

Toccata

Among Kapsberger's works, the toccatas show the boldest ventures into the new era. The one I have chosen, from the *Libro Primo D'Intavolatura di Chitarone* (Venice, 1604), is actually one of his more conservative. Unlike most, it is in the form of a series of arpeggios, much like the lute preludes of Weiss. In the original manuscript the arpeggiation pattern is not indicated and so is left to the performer's invention. The two recordings that I have heard each use a different pattern. Paul O'Dette plays a simple pima-pima-pima-pima for each chord while Hopkinson Smith uses the more complex pimi-aimi-paim-paim. The unusual tuning of the chitarrone and the ingenuity with which Kapsberger exploits it render both these patterns kaleidoscopic and even hypnotic. Most guitarists have some familiarity with Renaissance lute tuning, which is (as transposed for guitar) EAdf#be'; only the third string differs from the guitar. The chitarrone is the same with an insidious twist: The top two courses are tuned down an octave making it (again transposed for guitar) EAdf#Be. You can see that with a little rearranging to put them in ascending pitch order, the strings almost form a scale: EABdef#. As a result, what looks like an arpeggio in the tablature may actually be a cross-string scale. Another effect of the tuning, employed by Kapsberger in this toccata, is that many simple chord formations include unisons, so that the arpeggiation pattern is obscured. Unfortunately, this cannot be easily carried over into a guitar transcription and so I have made octave transpositions in these places. A couple of fingering comments: Measure 6 can be awkward. As with many such arpeggios, not all fingers need move at the same time. Also, note that by preparing in measure 5 as shown, the 3 and 4 fingers can remain in place for measure 6, leaving only the 1 and 2 fingers to move, one a time. Measure 31 has a long stretch. Again, preparation is the key, here with a two string partial barré, so that only the 3 and 4 fingers must move.

Gagliarda

The gagliarda ("galliard" in England) originated in Italy in the 16th century. It is a lively dance that intersperses 6/4 and 3/2 rhythms. In Kapsberger's fourth gagliarda from his *Libro Primo D'Intavolatura di Lauto* (Rome, 1611), transcribed here, this scheme adds a piquant hemiola to the dance. The only changes that I have made are a few chord re-voicings to make them guitar-friendly.

Corrente

Although the gagliarda did not survive into the Baroque period, the corrente did become one of the standard movements of the suite. The one transcribed here is charming, compact, and re-freshing. You may find that the lute fingering for scales, using thumb-index (pipi), works well for the sixteenth notes in the second half of the

Corrente. Measure 23 is a bit difficult but the indicated fingering will stabilize your left hand and facilitate the quick slurs.

If you have discovered a forgotten or defamed composer worthy of resurrection, or even a well-known one whose music merits transcription for the guitar, please let me know so that we can share it with the readers of future issues of *Soundboard*.

Three Short Pieces

Selected from music originally written for lute and chitarrone

Transcribed for guitar
by Richard Yates

G. G. Kapsberger
(c.1580–1651)

Toccata Arpeggiata (1604, chitarrone)

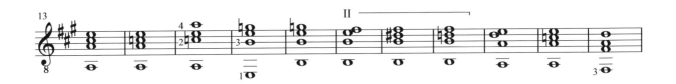

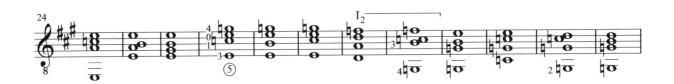

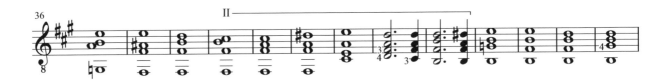

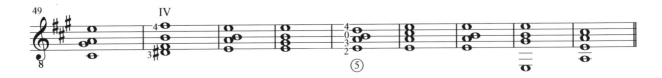

Gagliarda (1611, lute)

Corrente (1611, lute)

This page has been left blank to avoid awkward page turns.

See My Own Sweet Jewel and Thirsis

Thomas Morley

The story of Thomas Morley's life can be inferred only from fragmentary records. He was born in 1557 or 1558, and we have no other substantive information until, at the age of 25, he was appointed Master of Choristers at the cathedral in Norwich. There are tantalizing hints that he studied music with William Byrd for a couple of years as a teenager, but it is not until 1592—at the comparatively advanced age of 35—that he emerged as a well known musical figure with his appointment as a "Gentleman of the Chapel Royal." The following year the first of his published compositions appeared—*Canzonets or Little Short Songs to Three Voyces*. These were so well received that they elicited a large body of highly idiomatic music from a generation of composers known today as the English madrigalists. Morley composed in many forms and styles, but was most successful with madrigals and songs. In later years he involved himself in other musical endeavors such as editing and publishing, and he was the last person to hold the exclusive rights to publish music in England.

The *Canzonets*

The *Canzonets* take the form of three-voice, polyphonic songs in which the through-composed voices are woven into a texture that mixes homophonic and contrapuntal elements. The text is treated freely, with frequent repetitions and interpolations of words or phrases. Usually the text is adapted according to the needs of the counterpoint rather than the reverse—

a feature that suggests good opportunities for successful instrumental transcription. There is, of course, a centuries-old tradition of transcribing vocal music to fretted instruments. The early Renaissance lute repertoire contains many examples of intabulations of masses originally composed by such composers as Josquin des Pres and Guillaume Dufay. These are often unsatisfying, and they actually obscure rather than illuminate the essential qualities of the original. I have generally found the leap from voice to guitar to be the most difficult one to cross in making transcriptions. Often the voice's unique ability to sustain notes and connect a musical line does not survive this transition, but as you will see, Morley's *Canzonets* are unusual in this regard. There are many passages that seem natural to a fretted instrument and could be mistaken for simple translations of lute fantasias of the period.

Several features of this music make it suitable for transcription on the guitar. The pitch range is relatively narrow, allowing more choices of suitable key and fingering options. In fact, several pieces sit quite easily on only the top five strings of the guitar. It is a measure of Morley's skill that he invented delightful and varied counterpoint within such a limited range. Above all, the *Canzonets* have a rhythmic quality that helps project separate voices on a non-sustaining instrument. However, this feature also presents difficult questions as to both the layout of the score and performance of the music. The original publication was in the form of part-books, each part containing only a single line with no indications as to the movement of the other voices. This was a common way for such music to be printed; full scores were a luxury. In addition, the music is printed without bar lines.

Editorial Choices

Transposition

Because the pitch range of most of the *Canzonets* is not large, there are often several keys that are plausible candidates. I selected from among these with two goals in mind—first, to place the highest notes in the area between the fifth and tenth frets on the first string, and second, to use guitar-friendly keys that make the most of open strings in the many unisons that occur. A common hurdle in transcribing music to the guitar is the necessity of narrowing the range of the original music, often by raising sections of the bass line an octave. By contrast, in many places the *Canzonets* actually allow the option of lowering the bass relative to the top lines. I have made sparing use of this technique where it solved technical difficulties, preferring to keep the three voices at their original relative pitches. One result is that several pieces have no notes at all on the sixth string.

Only two of the *Canzonets* required the guitar's range to be extended by tuning the sixth string to a low D.

Tempo

The original scores have no tempo markings. The first reference in selecting a tempo should be the lyrics. These will usually give you a good sense of the mood of the piece, although they are not an infallible guide. You will find that the challenge of sustaining three contrapuntal voices often places a practical upper limit on the tempo, while the lower limit is usually imposed by the guitar's lack of sustain as compared to the voice.

Bar lines

Placing all three voices on one staff can be accomplished with careful layout, and results in textures familiar to guitarists, but the issue of bar lines is more complicated. Bar lines in music of this period had a more limited function than they do today. Often, their purpose was solely to give an occasional vertical alignment of the voices. Bar lines still serve this function today, but are also intimately connected with the concept of meter, that is, a regularly recurring pattern of beats. Today a bar line signals that a strong beat follows; it did not necessarily mean this in the Renaissance period. Adding bar lines in a modern transcription is necessary, but runs the risk of being over-interpreted. This is especially true with some Renaissance music, such as several of the *Canzonets*, in which the pattern of beats is flexible. One solution is to analyze the music, tracing the meter as it changes and showing changing time signatures within the piece. Edmund Fellowes' 1913 edition of the *Canzonets* used this method.

I have not followed this path for several reasons. First, many of the meter changes are subtle or ambiguous; the distinction between a meter change and an agogic accent can be very equivocal. Also, making time signature changes could further increase the player's unwarranted reliance on them as the map of beats, and lead him or her to overlook other accents. Last, the meter changes in the *Canzonets* are both infrequent and brief. Nearly all of them involve three 4/4 measures being divided into 3/4 + 3/4 + 3/2 (in the Fellowes edition). These changes are not long enough to create a regular pattern and are, in my opinion, best understood as a syncopation of the prevailing pattern of 4/4. My decision, therefore, was to add regular bar lines, but not to insert time signature changes. Players should keep this in mind and take care not to infer too much about accents from the bar lines. In the end, I do not think that there is much risk of error. The music, once heard a few times, announces its intentions quite clearly regardless of our fretting over notation minutiae.

Note durations

The next editorial decision concerned the durations of notes. While the *Canzonets* sit remarkably well on the guitar, there are still many places where notes in one voice or another cannot be sustained for their full duration. While this is a common problem in creating transcriptions, it is all the more so with Renaissance contrapuntal music. In transcribed guitar music, the most common notation shows notes shortened as they actually sound rather than with their original lengths. This gives a more accurate prescription of how to play a passage, but it also forces the player to deduce the original voices. My editorial choice was to preserve all of the note durations as they appear in the original, for the following reason: The original music is not known to performers, and most will not have access to the original to make comparisons. Therefore, I see a higher than usual value in preserving original note durations in the notation. By contrast, I would be more likely to present a guitar edition of a Bach fugue with note durations altered to coincide with specific and detailed fingerings. Also, many, perhaps even most, players make changes to fingerings based on preference or necessity. In this music there are many passages with plausible alternate fingerings. Selecting those that work best for me could limit the usefulness of this edition for other players. Including the original durations allows each player to make fully informed decisions in selecting fingerings that work best for him or her.

Fingerings

Polyphonic textures demand a careful analysis of musical requirements and technical possibilities, many of which are not apparent at first glance. I have found that the *Canzonets* contain numerous puzzles about to how to sustain the voices and, where they cannot all be held, which ones to sustain. Remarkably, the notes that cannot be sustained are quite rare, so persevere in seeking solutions; they are there waiting to be found. Preserving one note's duration may call for different fingering several beats earlier. So, although the fingerings in this transcription are fairly sparse, I have included those I believe will be helpful. Please keep in mind that the fingerings are entirely advisory; they should in no way be construed as showing the only, or even the best, way to play a passage. A large part of the pleasure of learning this music is found in the thoughtful consideration of these issues and the selection of fingerings that best balance the individual's musical expression and technical ability. I have designed this transcription to allow the player the latitude to experience this.

Lyrics

When approaching the transcription of a vocal work one is confronted with an immediate and obvious problem: what to do about the lyrics. Vocal music lyrics are certainly an essential feature that cannot be retained in a solo instrumental version. Inevitably, something is lost, but a skilled performer can mitigate this through familiarity with the text, so that its spirit, if not the exact words, can be projected. Also, Morley uses word repetition and the interweaving of voices to create not so much a narrative as an articulated texture. This can be replicated by the instrumental performer through careful attention to the articulation of notes. To help you imbue your performance with the spirit of the text, I have included lyrics for two of the *Canzonets*. Note that these are not the literal setting of the lyrics but, rather, are reductions that eliminate word repetition and interpolation and use modern spelling and punctuation.

1.

See my own sweet jewel, what I have for my darling:
A robin red breast and a starling.
These I give, both, in hope to move thee.
Yet thou say I do not love thee.

The first of the *Canzonets for Three Voices*, *See My Own Sweet Jewel*, is bright and witty. A quicker tempo and sharp articulation will convey the right spirit. From the start, this piece catches our attention through interesting rhythms. The Fellowes edition inserts time signature changes in the opening phrase: 4/4, 3/4, 3/2. There are identical groupings at measures 12, 29, and 40. In measure 19, the D in the middle voice cannot be sustained for its full written duration. This flaw is a minor one because the outer voices are intact and because the harmony does not change as it would in, for instance, a suspension.

12.

Thirsis, let some pity move thee,
Thou knowest thy Cloris too well doth love thee,
Then why, o dost thou fly me?
I faint, alas, here must I lie me,
Cry now for grief since he has bereft thee,
Up the hills, down the dales thou sets, dear, I have not left thee.
Ah can these trickling tears, these tears of mine, not procure love?
What shepherd ever killed a nymph for pure love?
See, cruel, see the beasts, see their tears they do reward me,
Yet thou dost not regard me.

Thirsis, Let Pity Move Thee was the first of the *Canzonets* to come to my attention. Its beauty and elegance, and the ease with which it fit the guitar prompted the search for the rest. It remains my favorite of the whole collection. Although it is modest in all literal and figurative dimensions, it develops slowly without drawing attention to itself, and the last line has a quiet and easily overlooked, yet somehow immense, depth.

The sixteenth notes on the second page caution against more than a moderate tempo and if necessary, the paired sixteenth notes at measures 45 and 55 may be modified by leaving out the ones in the bass voice. In measure 9, the 3 finger remains on the third string B note while the 4 finger moves down to the F sharp. The fingering in measure 66 allows the top F sharp to be sustained for its written duration.

References and Resources

Morley, Thomas, *Canzonets for Two and Three Voices*, Fellowes, Edmund Horace, ed., Stainer & Bell, London, 1913.

Morley, Thomas, *Canzonets or Little Short Songs to Three Voyces*, 39093 Performers' Facsimiles, New York, 1989.

Uhler, John Earle, *Morley's Canzonets for Three Voices*, Louisiana State University Press, Baton Rouge, 1957.

The entire set of twenty *Canzonets* is available for free at my web site: www.yatesguitar.com.

See My Own Sweet Jewel

Transcribed for guitar
by Richard Yates

Thomas Morley
(1557–1602)

Thirsis, Let Pity Move Thee

Transcribed for guitar
by Richard Yates

Thomas Morley
(1557–1602)

Rigaudon and Trio

Edvard Grieg

It is becoming downright unpleasant that my compositions are being disseminated in all kinds of arrangements. All that is lacking is a Peer Gynt Suite *for flute and bassoon.... Thank God I am totally innocent in all this.* —Edvard Grieg, 1896

When working on a transcription I sometimes ask myself: What would the composer think? How would he alter this if he were adapting it to the guitar? While these questions are unanswerable fantasies, and possibly only a psychological crutch, they can help direct attention to the style and practices of the period and to the particular composer, weighing what is essential to preserve. However, Grieg's quote above might give us pause rather than reassurance for making the attempt. But a bit more research shows the source of his frustration, and suggests that he might even approve. The *Peer Gynt Suite* was assembled from incidental music Grieg composed for Henrik Ibsen's play and was published in 1888. It was an immediate worldwide sensation. Demand was so fierce that the piece soon appeared in a bewildering variety of arrangements. Grieg's exasperation appears to be directed not so much at the arrangements per se, but rather at the particularly unsuitable vehicles onto which the music was sometimes forced. And the trend continues—today I found an arrangement of Grieg for steel band!

Historically, my own approach to transcription began with extreme caution. I was unsatisfied with the relative paucity of contrapuntal works for guitar, and so started with J. S. Bach. While his music has certainly been a mainstay of the guitar repertoire, the transcriptions did not come easily. Bach's music is a monument to be approached with reverence, and I was reluctant to transcribe anything that could not be transferred without modification. An equal obstacle was the rigor with which he composed: There is little that is arbitrary or padded; every note seems to have an essential purpose. However, a few pieces eventually worked out. One of them, a prelude from *The Well Tempered Clavier*, became the subject of the first *The Transcriber's Art* column in 1995. Over the years, with more experience and feedback from players, I find that I have loosened up considerably; I have greater confidence in making what are apparently more significant changes. I say "apparently" because I think I have a better appreciation for which elements are superficial and which are essential as I translate from one instrument to another. I am increasingly comfortable with a standard that looks primarily at the result and appraises it as it stands, without reference to the original. A transcription is music just as much as the original is, and it can be judged and enjoyed on its own merits. This installment of *The Transcriber's Art* includes a transcription that illustrates this approach.

The Composer

Edvard Hagerup Grieg (1843–1907) occupies a position in music history between Chopin and Debussy. Like Chopin, his best works were written for piano and are short, lyrical, and intimate, with a poignant harmonic sense. Both composers drew heavily from the folk melodies of their homelands: Chopin from Poland, Grieg from Norway. In later years Grieg's harmonic experiments approached the impressionism of Debussy. Indeed, Debussy used Grieg's string quartet as a model for his own. Regular readers of this column know of my predilection for the music of Chopin as a source for guitar transcriptions, and I am finding Grieg to be a deep wellspring as well. In particular, his 10 books of *Lyric Pieces* contain a wealth of attractive music that could keep transcribers busy for years.

Holberg Suite

This issue's featured transcription comes not from the *Lyric Pieces*, but from a larger scale work that is best known in its orchestral form, the suite *From Holberg's Time, Opus 40*. In December of 1884, the city of Bergen planned a bicentennial celebration of the birth of the Norwegian poet and playwright, Ludvig Holberg (1684–1754), who was an almost exact contemporary of J. S. Bach. Grieg eagerly accepted the challenge and produced a remarkable work. The composer said about the suite, "Once in a while it is a good exercise to conceal one's own individuality," but he was not completely successful in this. Firmly based on the French dance suite and Rococo style, the suite nevertheless is imbued with subtle touches of 19th century harmony and Griegian lyricism.

Although all of the suite's movements work on the guitar, I have chosen the *Rigaudon and Trio* for closer examination, as there are several aspects of the transcription that readers may find of interest. The illustrations that you see are from the piano version (transposed) made by Grieg himself.

A problem for the guitarist presents itself almost immediately. The first measure is comprised of an arpeggio in parallel octaves, with running eighth notes in both hands a bit later.

Figure 1

A lively tempo is necessary, so something must be done. Parallel octaves are a pianistic device and are usually awkward on the guitar (Wes Montgomery notwithstanding), and figures like those in measure five are difficult as well. The solution is clear once we relax any slavish fidelity to the original. The off-beat A notes are simply dropped, leaving a thoroughly idiomatic guitar texture. Similarly, the lower line in measure five is actually a compound line that combines a pedal point on A off the beat with a moving figure on the beat. Clearly the moving line is essential, while the pedal will scarcely be missed as it is duplicated an octave higher in the top line. Again, the result is a guitar-friendly texture that sacrifices little.

The next puzzle crops up at measure 15 in a descending sequence with overlapping lines.

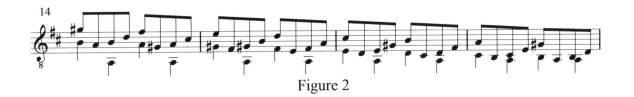

Figure 2

While it is possible to play the notes as written, the pitch gets perilously low for the guitar, and there is no fingering that will keep the voice leading distinct where there is overlap. A simple alteration to the top voice figure solves both problems. We lose the characteristic leap down a seventh, but the replacement is entirely suitable, both contrapuntally and practically. My estimation is that, without knowing the original, knowledgeable listeners would have no idea that the line had been modified. The transcription is entirely idiomatic to the period and the instrument.

Measure 27 presented a larger problem. In the original, the phrase here is nearly identical to the one immediately preceding it, except that it is a full octave higher. Only a small percentage of guitarists—certainly not including myself—might be able to play this phrase up around the 17th fret, but there are other options. What about simply repeating the phrase without the octave transposition? This is the obvious solution, but is an example of preserving what is superficial at the expense of what is essential. For me, what is essential in this phrase is that it repeats the harmonic progression of the preceding phrase, and that it is in a higher pitch range. So, while it is impractical to go up the full octave, a revoicing of the chords so that the moving line is on the top rather than in the middle provides a similar effect and preserves the function of the phrase within the structure of the piece as a whole.

Rigaudon and Trio

Holberg Suite, Op. 40

Transcribed for guitar
by Richard Yates

Edvard Grieg
(1843–1907)

Fantasia XV

Giovanni Battista della Gostena

It is better to know some of the questions than all of the answers. —James Thurber

The second half of the 16th century was a remarkable time in music history. The developments of the previous 100 years had refined and polished the High Renaissance style to an unprecedented degree of sophistication and complexity. The lute was fully involved in these trends and, pushed by the music's increasing technical demands, approached the limit of its potential. In subsequent years, the instrument itself needed modifications in order to keep up.

Renaissance lute music is an endless source for transcriptions for guitar, but much of it can be found only in the original tablature format. Many classical guitarists have reservations, or even alarm, about the proliferation of modern tablature for guitar music in magazines and on the Internet. I find it interesting that in the lute world there is a similar, if inverted, controversy about the advisability of making pitch notation transcriptions rather than reading from the original tablature. Even more heat is generated about the best way to do this. As the present article is written for guitarists, I am sidestepping the first of these disputes and focusing on the second. Yet, even this narrowing of the topic leaves a tangle of issues. Note that this will not be an explanation of how to decode the symbols of the varieties of tablature—that topic is thoroughly addressed in many references. Instead, I will introduce other problems that a guitarist must face in making a transcription from lute tablature. I must also disavow any pretension of complete treatment of this topic. My hope is to describe clearly the puzzles and possible solutions that arise in the course of making a particular transcription from the Renaissance lute repertoire. I believe that you will find that the themes illustrated in these examples recur in any attempts that you make at the lute music of this period.

Historically, there has been a range of approaches. You will find an informative essay, *A History of Transcriptions of Lute Tablature, 1679 to the Present,* written by Matanya Ophee and posted at his website, http://www.orphee.com/trans/trans.html. Discussions about tablature transcription tend to polarize into two approaches: literal versus interpretive. However, in practice, these categories are not so clear-cut and transcriptions fall along a continuum. Yet, even this conceptualization is not entirely adequate to capture the complexity of the issues. An illustration may help.

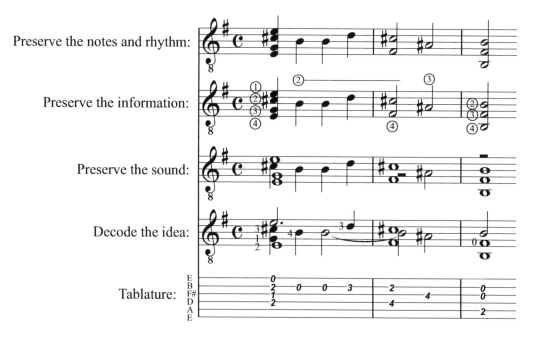

Preserve the notes and rhythm:

Preserve the information:

Preserve the sound:

Decode the idea:

Tablature:

Figure 1, measures 7–9

Figure 1 shows four different transcriptions of one tablature staff. For convenience, the tablature staff has been translated from the original Italian lute tablature into modern guitar tablature, including transposition down a minor third. String tuning is shown at the left; the highest pitched string is the top one and numbers show the fret where a note is fingered. As you can see, the tuning uses that of the Renaissance lute, in which the third string is a half step lower (F sharp) than normal guitar tuning.

The top staff contains only information that can be directly obtained from the tablature notation itself. This version actually has less information than the original as the assignment of particular notes to strings has been omitted. Tablature gives only partial information about note durations—it shows the point at which each note begins, but unless a subsequent note falls on the same string, the ending time of the note is unspecified. This type of transcription, although it conveys less than the original, is what is generally referred to as a "literal" transcription. Ophee calls it "Schrade notation"

after Leo Schrade who used it in the 1920s. It preserves only the pitches and the rhythm.

The second staff preserves only the information in the original tablature. While it is not a practical notation, it does demonstrate the efficient use of space—one of the useful characteristics of tablature.

The third staff takes more of the context into account. Specifically, it recognizes that some notes are able to sound longer and that the common practice is to let them do so. This version infers and combines information from the notation, the physical configuration of the instrument, and the typical manner of playing it; it is an interpretive approach that preserves the sound.

The standard notation staff at the bottom takes the process of inference a step further. It recognizes the broader context of the musical style and the period in which the music is composed. While these inferences are more speculative than those about the instrument itself, many can be made with a high degree of confidence. Music of this period had a thoroughly developed and coherent style and many of its features were quite conventional. This staff decodes and displays the musical idea.

Which of these is correct or proper? My view is that all of them can be, depending on the purpose for which they are used. Even the monstrosity on the second staff could have a hypothetical, legitimate context: It is the only version that communicates the precise information in the tablature without omissions or additions. My purpose is to produce performing scores for classical guitarists that are practical and readable—that balance the visual presentation of the musical ideas with performance instructions. This means that the resulting score may not fit neatly into one of the categories illustrated in Figure 1, but then, nearly all transcriptions mix approaches to some extent. The basic task of transcription is to preserve that which is essential. Sometimes it also means adding that which is beautiful based on the different resources of the new medium.

Because the goal is an edition for a different instrument, the transcriber must consider the notational peculiarities of music written for that instrument. Guitar music notation has been subject to wide swings of opinion and practice that have by no means been entirely resolved. While some guitarists look askance at modern tablature's spotty information about note durations, they would do well to remember that standard guitar notation is far from a paradigm of precision. Bass notes are often allowed and intended to ring longer than their written durations. Similarly, the sound of arpeggio textures bears little resemblance to a literal performance of the notes. So in making transcriptions we must remember that we are translating from one fuzzy notation to another. In addition, we need to understand the technical aspects of performance on the original instrument, but also recognize the differences between the original and destination instrument.

Finally, music has always been notoriously difficult to proofread, and the scores that have reached us from the 16th century are no exception. Detection and correction of notation errors requires interpretation and consideration of the musical and stylistic context.

With this thin introduction complete, we can now see how these ideas are applied in the nitty-gritty of transcribing tablature.

Giovanni Battista della Gostena

Giovanni Battista della Gostena (c. 1540–1598) was an Italian composer and lutenist. His musical resume includes an apprenticeship under Philippe de Monte (1521–1603) and an appointment as maestro di cappella at the Cathedral of San Lorenzo in Genoa. He was the uncle and teacher of another distinguished lutenist-composer, Simone Molinaro (c. 1565–c. 1634). Gostena's published compositions include, in addition to lute works, the standard vocal forms of the period: madrigals, motets, and magnificats. His credentials as a composer will bear on some puzzles that we will soon encounter.

Fantasia XV Questions

The transcription we will examine is of a piece published in 1599 as part of a collection of dances and fantasias by Gostena and Molinaro. The title of "fantasia" has been used for a wide and disparate variety of music over the centuries. In 16th century Italy it was an instrumental form for keyboard or lute, often of a highly imitative texture. The turn of the century was the peak for both Renaissance polyphonic complexity and the advancement of lute technical capabilities. Some music of this time succeeds remarkably and some falls somewhat short but is no less glorious for the attempt. Gostena's lute music presents an even greater number of puzzles for the transcriber. Some of these defy definitive explanation, but our attempts at resolving them can, nonetheless, be educational.

An early question faced by the transcriber of lute tablature is this: How many voices comprise this music? Examination of the whole tablature score shows clearly that, although the texture is quite contrapuntal, there is not a consistent number of voices throughout. Certainly, contrapuntal technique often uses, and even relies on, the intermittent dropping out of voices, but in this fantasia voices appear and disappear more often than that. Generally, the texture uses three or four voices but, as can be seen right from measure 1, it is inconsistent, and rather puzzlingly so.

Figure 2, measures 1–4

Looking first at just the tablature staff, we see a homophonic texture in which some chords have three notes and some have four. The phrase is simple and beautiful, and strongly suggests the choral settings with which Gostena was familiar, and yet the number of voices is not consistent. Of course, it is routine to see lute or guitar music in which four-voice texture cannot be sustained and can be only implied. What is most curious here is that the voices could have been included in a thoroughly idiomatic and correct way, one that highlights a unique capability of the lute— the ability to play genuine unisons in chords on a solo instrument. Indeed, the two chords with only three notes both have interior open strings for which unisons are readily available. Why did Gostena not use them? Setting this question to the side for the moment, you can see that my choice has been to fill out the chords.

Measures 7 and 8 present an enigma that embodies all the themes recounted earlier. They are shown in Figure 1. The music is interpreted as a 4–3 suspension. This is a common, even endemic, cadential formula of this period and style. Here, the cadence rounds out the period in which the first phrase ends with a similar 4–3 suspension. It is not the least bit speculative to read it this way. And yet, in Gostena's tablature the suspended note, B in this key, is abruptly silenced by the D that is played on the second string at the last beat of measure 7. Why did he not arrange the fingering as shown in the transcription, where he could, with little added difficulty, carry out the obvious musical intention? This is a second question that will not be taken up until we inspect some other puzzles.

In measure 28 the problem is again related to sustaining voices. Here the top staff shows how the music would sound as notated in tablature. In an idealized version the top voice would be suspended into the first beat of measure 8, but there is no way to then play the three notes that follow on the first string. The second staff shows a reasonable way to include the suspended A note. The cost is to subsequently interfere with the E note on the second string. But there is an acoustic effect that mitigates this cost: The bass note is the open sixth string E note. The pitch of the second string E note is well represented in the overtones of the bass note, so much so that the higher E note is hardly audible when cut off by the melody. The lowest standard notation staff shows the version I used in my transcription. It is the second staff without the niggling detail showing rests where the higher E note is silenced. This makes a less cluttered score and

71

Figure 3, measures 27–28

is actually a more accurate representation of the sound. In any event, I would choose to preserve the melody at the expense of an interior supporting voice rather than the opposite. Why did Gostena not also do this?

Rather than risk losing the remaining readers who have persevered through these minutiae I will simply highlight a few more places with the questions they evoke and omit the analysis.

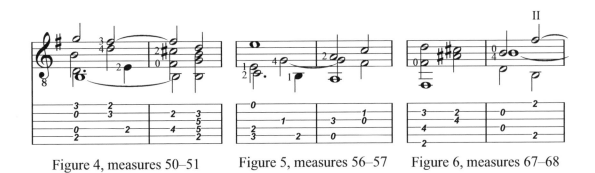

Figure 4, measures 50–51   Figure 5, measures 56–57   Figure 6, measures 67–68

Measure 51: Why place the F sharp on the fourth string when it can more easily be played on the third?

Measure 57: Why cut off the suspended G note when it can be sustained using another fingering without affecting other notes?

Measure 67: Again, why not use the open third string for the F sharp?

Measure 68: Why not maintain the three-voice texture when it would be easy and appropriate to do so?

Answers?

For a couple of pages I have been focusing on questions and sidestepping answers. If you have been hoping for an authoritative and enlightening epiphany at this point then you may be disappointed. I do not have a magic key that unlocks these puzzles, but there are some possibilities that may be of interest and perhaps helpful when you either read or produce transcriptions of tablature.

The edition from which the *Fantasia* was drawn was published after Gostena's death in 1598. As he was not around to make corrections, it is possible that errors crept in during the production of the book. On the other hand, the publisher was actually his nephew, Simone Molinaro, a person unlikely to have made such errors.

In some of the enigmatic spots, the more musically complete version is simply harder to play. Perhaps Gostena was aiming to minimize the difficulty level. This is also a less than satisfying answer, as the level of difficulty of many of the fantasias is rather high, and some of the apparently better fingerings are even easier than the tablature.

Perhaps the inferences I have made about the music are simply wrong and the voice leading is entirely as intended. This is certainly possible; there is lute music from this period written by composers who knew only the lute and who may have lacked formal training. Of course, what we know of Gostena's credentials suggests that would be farfetched in his case.

The last possibility that has occurred to me is simply carelessness in preparing the manuscript. Perhaps the better fingerings were just overlooked. The erratic distribution of questionable fingerings supports this. Many places are carefully fingered to sustain notes or to preserve the number of voices, while others are not. This carelessness might have been more likely to happen if the tablature was not the original notation in which the music was composed, but was simply a transcription itself! This idea coincides with an intriguing speculation by Arthur Ness, the editor of the landmark edition of *The Lute Music of Francesco da Milano (1497–1543), Volumes I and II*. It may be that a substantial amount of lute music in tablature was originally composed in pitch notation and then subsequently intabulated by the composer. We know that it was a common practice of the period to do this with existing choral works. Indeed, the edition from which the *Fantasia* was drawn includes such intabulations of originals by prominent composers Thomas Créquillon (1480–1557), Orlando di Lasso (c. 1532–1594), and Clemens non Papa (c. 1510–c. 1556). Further, if fragmentary, support for this hypothesis occurs in several other places in Gostena fantasias, where the tablature is actually impossible to play yet is musically correct. If these are not simply typographical errors that happen to sound right, how else would they occur except by faulty intabulation of an existing pitch notation score? I do not know of any works written in pitch notation and then later set in tablature by the same composer, but it seems likely that this would not have been an unusual practice, and Gostena certainly had the facility to work in both notation systems.

While this perusal of a particular tablature score offers no conclusive answers, I hope that the resulting questions and conjectures have shed light on the complexity of the transcription process, and directed attention to important issues to consider in bringing the music of this marvelous period within the reach of today's guitarists.

Fantasia XV

(1599)

Transcribed for guitar
by Richard Yates

G. B. della Gostena
(c. 1540–1598)

This page has been left blank to avoid awkward page turns.

Prelude, Op. 81, No. 20
Stephen Heller

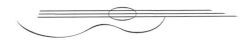

Iusually discover music to transcribe by sifting through scores or recordings looking and listening for the features I have often discussed in these columns. However, I recently found an abundant source through a different means. It started with just the name of a composer of whom I had never heard: Stephen Heller. A bit of investigation turned up these few facts; he was a prolific 19th century composer, quite familiar to piano students, and best known for smaller musical forms such as preludes and studies. This meager information was enough to spur me to order, sight unseen, three collections of Heller's music. The small gamble paid off, as I found a high proportion of the pieces quite suitable for the guitar. One of those is this issue's featured transcription.

Stephen Heller

Born in Hungary in 1813, he began piano lessons and, as his talent became apparent, moved up through a series of teachers until he went to Vienna to study with Carl Czerny. By the time he was 15 years old he was ready for a two-year concert tour through Eastern Europe. This ended in Augsburg where, exhausted, he stayed for eight years, working under the patronage of Frau Caroline Hoeslin von Eichthal and Count Friedrich Fugger-Kirchem-Hoheneck. His compositions received the enthusiastic support of Robert Schumann. Heller moved to Paris in 1938 and lived there the remainder of his life, composing, teaching, and writing musical criticism.

The list of his compositions is long, covering about 160 opus numbers, many consisting of several pieces. His studies and preludes have established themselves in the piano literature. I would recommend to anyone looking for fresh transcription sources:

> 25 *Études Faciles, opus 45*
> 25 *Études Pour Former au Sentiment*
>   *du Rythme et á L'expression, opus 47*
> 32 *Préludes à Mlle. Lili, opus 119*
> 24 *Préludes, opus 81*

The studies in *opus 16* and *opus 46* seemed promising but were discontented and uncomfortable on the guitar. Perhaps someone else can discover a more efficacious transcription than I was able to. In Heller's work you will find familiar 19th century harmonic language, graceful if not memorable melodies, and interesting, attractive, and inventive rhythms. The pitch ranges, harmonic complexity and voicing density are nearly always of a scope that allows successful transcription to the guitar.

Prelude, Op. 81, No. 20

Originally in the key of C minor, this prelude is marked *con espressione di dolore amaro* ("with expression of bitter pain"). Lest this heading scare off guitarists, please note that the sentiment it evokes for me is rather softer, and the mood improves as the piece proceeds. As with many of Heller's preludes, a small number of measures encompasses a varied series of narrative events that is almost operatic. Here are some of the highlights:

Measure 1

A descending melodic interval has been used for

centuries to signal a less than cheerful mood. Heller enhances this effect in the first two beats by making the melodic interval a tritone, creating minor third harmonic intervals on both notes and avoiding the tonic by outlining an ambiguous dominant seventh chord which disorients the listener. With so much emotional baggage built into the notes, how could I resist fingering them with lots of vibrato on the top end and a glissando connecting them? Use a little restraint in how long you make the glissando, but if even this is not enough bitter pain for you, try the melody on the third string. In the original piano score the figure is doubled at the octave in the left hand—a texture that can usually be simplified without damage to the music.

Measure 7

Note that the barré can be placed on the second fret without lifting the 4 finger from the A note on the first string. This difficulty is worth being able to connect the A note to the following B flat. The opening figure reappears, but with a compressed form and in the subdominant key.

Measure 13

Again, the top note of the chord can be held, although the stretch may thwart some players. Of course, we are now even further from the tonic, apparently, at least by analogy, headed for E minor.

Measure 20

The harmonic ambiguity begins to clear. The theme appears again but here, significantly, descends down a perfect fifth, without the depressive minor thirds. Remarkably, from this point on, the harmony remains strictly and solidly in the tonic key. Only notes of the harmonic minor scale are used. Although still in a minor key, the emotional expression is lighter, more open, perhaps more wistful or melancholic than bitter.

Measure 22

The echo of measure 20 is rendered effectively using *ponticello*.

Measure 23

The same texture continues from here to measure 32. It is important to keep the melody singing in the foreground and the accompaniment understated—its main purpose, not yet apparent, is its rhythm. The duple rhythm of the accompaniment interferes, in the wave sense, with the motion of the 9/8 meter.

Measure 32

With what has preceded harmonically, and especially rhythmically, Heller has set up a marvelous moment. The hobbled rhythmic movement flows freely once again. There is release and consolation in the grief …

Measure 34

… and possibly even some hope. The dynamic marking preserved in the transcription indicates crescendo all the way to a *sforzando* at measure 35. Personally, I like to play the peak of this line, the first beat of measure 35, *subito piano*, that is, "suddenly softer." This can make the top notes float out ethereally. The sixth string, twelfth fret, natural harmonic adds to this effect, and is also convenient for sustaining the sound over the shift down on the second beat.

I think you will enjoy playing this little jewel from Stephen Heller, but I would be especially happy to hear from readers who might attempt other Heller pieces. If you have such contributions to make, please get in touch.

Prelude
Op. 81, No. 20

Transcribed for guitar
by Richard Yates

Stephen Heller
(1813–1888)

Molto Lento *(con espressione di dolore amaro)*

Fugue 17
The Well-Tempered Clavier, Book I
Johann Sebastian Bach

The rosebush, a castoff from a neighbor in the midst of garden redesign, leaned against the fence, balanced unsteadily in its wrapped and bound root ball. As it was certainly too large and dense of habit for the modest corner I had available, I set about planting and pruning; I removed the unnecessary stems, cut back its extension to fit the setting, and thinned the interwoven structure to let in the air and the light.

In this installment of *The Transcriber's Art* I will attempt to grasp the thorny issues involved in reshaping a paragon of contrapuntal art. Although there may be an air of sacrilege about this enterprise, the purists have likely long ago abandoned this series of articles and those readers who remain may obtain a delicate and attractive addition for that vacant corner in their repertoires.

The music under consideration is *Fugue 17* from the first book of J. S. Bach's *The Well-Tempered Clavier*. This famous collection, together with Book 2, of 48 paired preludes and fugues in all keys is a timeless bouquet with the deserved status of a precious heirloom. All of Bach's music has been gleaned for those pieces that can be adapted to the guitar, and the books of *The Well Tempered Clavier* are no exception. The obstacles are great, however, especially with the fugues. The continuous voice lines in three and four parts have even challenged generations of keyboard players despite their instruments' considerable technical advantages in managing such textures. Careful selection is advised.

Fugue 17, BWV 862, appeared to be especially suited to cultivation for the guitar. Although it is nominally a four-voice fugue, the texture is frequently thinner. Nearly two-thirds of the measures have an essentially three-part texture and the third voice often moves in long half notes that serve only to fill in harmony notes, providing background for prominent motion in the other two parts. Further examination, especially listening to a harpsichord performance, reinforces this observation from the score. For instance, the moderate tempo, relatively rapid decay of notes, and attention-grabbing movement of other voices ensure that although half notes are melodically connected, the actual sound has bloomed and faded long before the next note. As we will see later, this feature will help simplify both the music notation and the fingering, because many notes will not have to be sustained for their written durations.

I find it useful to begin by defining the parameters within which to work, that is, what in the original is inviolate and what is permissible to transform? By establishing such ground rules the result can be consistent and coherent throughout the transcription. In this fugue I thought it essential to preserve the entries and note durations of the fugue theme. I have also set them off visually in the notation of note stems. When the texture required pruning, I cut back the most subsidiary voices first so that the thematic structure was preserved.

As is typical, the range of the original music exceeds the guitar's three and a half octaves, and so the usual transpositions are necessary. Fugues, by their nature, can be awkward on a fretted instrument, yet there are a couple of characteristics evident in this piece that mitigate some of the difficulties.

First is the issue of contrapuntal inversion. Fugue themes are most useful when they are invertible with their counterpoint. This means that either voice can sit in the higher pitched range without violating the rules of harmony and counterpoint. A fugue can thus unfold by placing the theme in different voices and pitch ranges. This characteristic nicely accommodates guitar transcribers' need to make octave transpositions. For example (see Figure 1), the entry of the middle voice on the second beat of measure six has been dropped relative to the lowest voice and the result is still an acceptable counterpoint. It is also true that this change to the original is a considerably more significant one than the common transcription practice of moving a bass line an octave closer to a melody without crossing it.

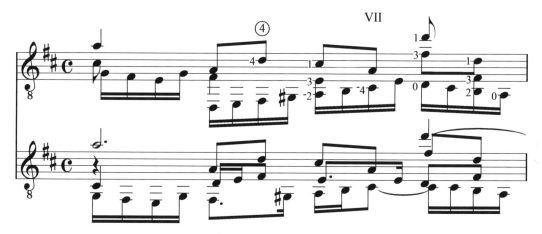

Figure 1, measure 6

Second, there are a few places in this fugue where two subsidiary lines comfortably combine into one (again see Figure 1). When the middle voice in the original is dropped down an octave it neatly meshes with the middle voice into a simple, idiomatic scale figure. In fact, this very figure occurs later in the fugue as a counterpoint to a modification of the theme (see measures 19–20) and helps validate hybridizing the two voices. It is tempting, though perhaps bordering on presumptuous, to speculate that this is how Bach himself derived the two lower voices. Having first conceived them as a single line, he then teased them apart into two.

Both of these alterations to the original, inversion of the counterpoint and reduction of the number of voices, have edged us past *transcription* and into the area of *arrangement* or even *recomposition*. For those readers with a conservative view, I have tried to do this gently in hopes that the result can be judged for what it is rather for what it is no longer.

In the graphical notation of this fugue I altered my usual practice. When adapting keyboard music to the six strings of the guitar, there frequently are notes that cannot be sustained for the duration indicated in the original. Having first decided how the music is to be played—that is, which notes must be shortened—the next task is to decide how to show this in the score. The choices are: 1) to show the notes shortened, as they will actually sound on the guitar, or 2) to leave the note durations as in the original, but to use fingering symbols to show how to actually play the passage. My preference has usually been to do the latter because it often makes the original melodic structure more clear. And also, the player may in fact discover a better way to hold the notes. The top line of measure six shows a simple example. There is no reasonable way to hold the A note for three beats, but even so, writing it as a dotted half note could better show that it is melodically connected to the high D on the last beat. However, in music as texturally dense as a fugue, there may be many such notes. Fingering is difficult enough without the additional burden on the player of resolving contradictions between indicated durations of notes and the fingering that does not sustain them.

I decided on this approach after looking at a transcription of another Bach solo—a version of the *Partita No. 1* for solo violin transcribed for … solo violin! Before our editor-in-chief can grab his red pencil, let me explain.

Figure 2

The lower staff is how the music is notated in Bach's manuscript; the upper staff is the edition, still available, by Josef Joachim, a renowned violinist of the last century. As you can see from the example, Joachim shortens the written duration of notes to more closely match the actual sound when the music is played. The curved arrangement of the strings of a violin, together with the firm tension in the bow, prevents more than two notes from being played at once. Larger chords must be rapidly arpeggiated with one stroke of the bow. For the first chord, you can see that the bottom three notes are written as eighth notes while only the top note is held for a full quarter. But even if Joachim's version is more accurate as to the resulting sound, why call it a "transcription"? Well, there is one school of historical research that hypothesizes that Bach's version was not notated as it is just because it was simpler to do it that way but, rather, the Baroque bow, with a looser stringing and tension modulated continuously by the thumb, may have allowed three and four notes to be played

simultaneously. There is an intriguing recording by Rudolf Gähler (*Arte Nova Classics*) in which he uses such a bow and quite successfully plays the Bach violin *Sonatas and Partitas* exactly as written. Despite this demonstration, the theory is a matter of some controversy, and certainly not one I intend to resolve. But correct or not, it provides an interesting model for the present fugue in that it suggests a manner of notating the music for an instrument that cannot sustain the note durations in the original score.

Just as none of us can create a rose, we cannot create a Bach fugue. But with care and knowledge of the species and its patterns of growth it is possible to adapt it to an agreeable setting so it may be seen and appreciated by a new audience. Whether you think that I have succeeded or awkwardly hacked up a prize-winner to cram into a pot on the window sill, please send in your comments and contributions.

Fugue 17

Well-Tempered Clavier, Book I

Transcribed for guitar
by Richard Yates

J. S. Bach
(1685–1750)

Sarabande con Variazioni

G. F. Handel

I know it when I see it. —Supreme Court Justice Potter Stewart, *Jacobellis v. Ohio* (1964)

Even the most thorough music reference books can be no more specific than to describe a folia as a "musical framework." Some sources emphasize the harmonic progression, although this can vary considerably; some highlight the melody, with similarly broad parameters. There are folias that carry the title, and those that do not. There are short ones and long ones; old ones and new ones; fast ones and slow ones; major mode and minor mode; square rhythmed and dotted; with an anacrusis and without; those starting on the tonic and on the dominant. The more examples one sees, the less clear are the boundaries. And yet, despite all this fog, there is undeniably something at the core that unites these pieces and that makes them robust enough to survive for the last 500 years.

The excellent article by Kurt Martinez in *Soundboard, Vol. XXX, No. 2,* documents the guitar's role in the folia saga, while I will discuss one example in a transcription for guitar.

Is Handel's *Sarabande* a Folia?

Rather than slowly sketch out the evidence bearing on this question to try to artificially create suspense about a new discovery, let me just say simply at the outset: Sure it is. This is not a deep musicological finding, and given the fuzzy boundaries of the class of pieces known as folia, it is not likely to receive a completely conclusive answer. But as we will see, Handel's *Sarabande* from the harpsichord *Suite in D Minor, (HWV 437)* has many features nearly identical to the Jean Baptiste Lully (1632–1687) version—considered the prototype for all that followed. Given this, it is a bit surprising that Handel is not mentioned in the long lists of famous composers who have written folias, and that at least one source explicitly disputes the assertion.

Lully's version is found in his *Air des hautbois, Les folies d'Espagne (LWV 48)* for four oboes, composed in 1672. The folia was so popular at the time that the king himself ordered this composition. The four-part setting begins like this, transposed for easy comparison to the key of my Handel transcription and in readable, if awkward, guitar notation:

Figure 1

Title

The title of the Handel piece does not disqualify it. Many folias have masqueraded under different names; in Italy they were known as *fedele* and in England as *Farinell's Ground*. The matching features of the folia and the sarabande were noted as early as 1717, well before Handel composed his in 1733. Lastly, the Handel piece is part of a Baroque dance suite in which a sarabande rather than a folia is mandatory.

Form

Both the Lully and the Handel pieces are in triple meter, in the key of D minor, by far the most common key for the later folia, and consist of 48 measures divided into a theme and two variations of 16 measures each. These in turn are constructed from two regular eight-measure phrases. Both sound best when played at a stately tempo. The typical rhythm in both pieces has a dotted value on the second beat of each measure, another characteristic of the later folia.

Harmonic Progression

This is a defining characteristic of the folia although, as I have mentioned, there was considerable variance from the standard formula over the centuries. It was common to interpolate other harmonies between the main structural ones. Figure 2 shows the progressions used by Lully and Handel:

Lully	i	V	i	VII (V of III)	III	VII	i	V
Handel	i	V	III	VII	iv	i	iv	V

Note that this analysis is only at the level of measures. In both pieces there are changes, often on the third beat, that smooth the transition to the next measure. The similarities are clear, and if there is any single characteristic of the folia's harmonic progression, it would have to be the majestic movement to the relative major. Handel merely gets there sooner and then draws out the return to the minor tonic.

Variations

Lully's scheme is simple: The first variation spins a continuous eighth-note melody in the top voice over identical harmonies and voicings in the lower three voices. The second variation does the same but the lowest voice has divisions. Handel's second variation follows the same pattern, if not the identical notes, as Lully's. His first variation is different, however. Indeed, it is much more complex and inventive. As you can see from the score, it is written in the *style brisé*, where fragments of lines enter and leave in an apparent, but not actual, counterpoint. This is of particular interest to guitarists since style brisé is thought to have originated in lute music, especially that of Denis Gaultier, and was only later adopted by the keyboardists. I have taken pains to duplicate the note durations, through both the notation and fingering, as they occur in the original.

So, aside from this theoretical analysis, what do you think? Does Handel's *Sarabande* have that folia feel? Will you be hearing echoes of it in a multitude of other compositions? Will you be humming it to yourself for the next 400 years? Then that's a folia!

Sarabande con Variazioni

Suite in D Minor, HWV 437

Transcribed for Guitar
by Richard Yates

G. F. Handel
(1685–1759)

Tendre Fleur and La Petite Réunion

Johann Friedrich Burgmüller

Regardless of the instrument, beginning music students must survive the ordeal of learning an endless series of short but dull compositions written by composers whose talents seem to lie solely in the painful exposing of players' technical weaknesses. Who of us did not, at one time or another, try to rationalize this gantlet with the half-hearted thought, "Well, if it were real music I probably wouldn't be able to concentrate as well on what my fingers are doing." If we were fortunate, and not too bored to notice, our curriculum may also have included music that excelled at being both musical and instructive. Many of the studies of Fernando Sor certainly fall into this category, in marked contrast to the tedium of those offered by lesser composers whom I will not name due to the, albeit minimal, risk of offending those who retain an irrational nostalgia for those early lessons.

It is interesting to compare the pedagogical literature of different instruments, for instance, the piano and guitar. On one hand there are similarities because the elements of music construction—such as scales, chords, and arpeggios—apply to both. But there are also differences that originate in the instruments' configurations themselves. You will find a dearth of artificial harmonics studies for the piano, or those perfecting the use of the sustaining pedal on the classical guitar. Careful consideration of this comparison is useful for the transcriber, as we can find piano studies that both teach and delight, and which maintain the lesson on the guitar without diminishing their beauty.

The Composer

Johann Friedrich Burgmüller (1806–1874) is a name that none of you will have heard unless you are a student of either obscure music history or the piano. He does not have an entry in the massive *New Grove Dictionary of Music and Musicians* and is mentioned only in relation to father and brother—but then, you have probably not heard of them either. In the other major biographical compendia you will find that he was born in Germany but settled in Paris about 1832 to teach and compose. Although he wrote one ballet, other stage works and "songs of little merit" (*New Grove*), he was best known for his sets of progressive piano studies and other pieces for children. These show a melodic gift and a talent for infusing technical lessons with musical interest.

I have been unable to find a complete list of his works, but if opus numbers are any indication, he was rather prolific. He seems to have hit his stride when he got up to triple digits: The best known studies are in the collections *Opus 100, 105,* and *109*. I have looked carefully at all 35 studies in these collections and discovered them to be a most fruitful source of material for transcription to the guitar. It is also evident that Burgmüller had a talent for writing charming melody in compact formats. Some editions are still in print after more than 100 years and you will find that many libraries still have them as well.

Opus 100

Twenty-five Easy and Progressive Studies for the piano has a subtitle that should immediately entice the guitarist: "Expressly Composed for Small Hands." A common hurdle in playing piano music on the guitar is not only the overall pitch range of the music, but also the size of the intervals and the number of notes at any given time. *Opus 100* seems, thankfully for guitarists, to have been composed for short arms as well as small hands. As a result, many of the studies can be transferred with minimal alterations. All of the pieces have the descriptive titles, common for 19th century character pieces, which announce the mood: *La Candeur, Innocence, La Pastorale*, etc.

La Petite Réunion

The fourth piece of this collection is a study in successions of thirds. A little experimentation at the keyboard and the fingerboard shows that the two instruments have related fingering issues in this musical context. Another interesting comparison to make is between Burgmüller's study and *Op. 6, No. 6* by Fernando Sor (*Estudio XII* in the Segovia edition).

The transcription of *La Petite Réunion* was straightforward—the only significant change was in measure 16, where the harmonic intervals of a third, in the original, have been inverted by lowering the top notes an octave. This was done to keep the difficulty level moderate and is consistent with the composer's occasional use of the interval of a sixth for variety, as seen in the closing two measures. One unusual fingering solution deserves mention: In measure seven, on the third beat, the 2 and 3 fingers are reversed from what would be their most natural arrangement in isolation. This was done in order to sustain the bass note for its full duration and facilitate its being heard as moving melodically up to the A note in the next measure. The fingering is easy with a little practice, as it uses both the 2 and the 4 fingers as guide fingers.

Tendre Fleur

The tenth study in *Opus 100* is an engaging exercise in counterpoint, with the attendant task of connecting and individually shaping two individual voices. This is most challenging in those sections where both voices move in eighth notes. To keep the sound from becoming choppy rather than flowing, accent the first and third beats. In fact, although the time signature is 4/4, the implicit meter of the music itself seems more like 2/2. The other technical objective of this study is in the use of staccato articulation, which I have carried over largely intact from the original.

I think you will enjoy playing these miniature lessons of Johann Friedrich Burgmüller, and I would be especially happy to hear from readers who might attempt his other works. If you have such contributions to make, please get in touch.

Tendre Fleur

Op. 100, No. 10

Transcribed for guitar
by Richard Yates

J. F. Burgmüller
(1806–1874)

La Petite Réunion

Op. 100, No. 4

Transcribed for guitar
by Richard Yates

J. F. Burgmüller
(1806–1874)

Sonata VIII

Johann Helmich Roman

The Baroque era has always been a favorite source of transcription material for guitarists, and hundreds of pieces have been garnered from the best-known masters. But as prolific as Bach, Handel, Telemann, and others were, one gets the impression that transcribers sometimes show more enthusiasm and wishful thinking than good judgment. They often stretch musical aesthetics and our instrument's technique in the quest to discover something new in these works. Rummaging through the music of lesser-known or obscure composers of the period—while less commercially valuable—can be interesting.

It was on such an expedition that I came across that master of the Swedish Baroque, Johann Helmich Roman. Hardly a household name these days outside of his home country, he was quite prominent in his time. Far from being a remote outpost, Sweden was solidly within the scope of the royalty round-robin by which alliances were forged and over which wars were waged. Aside from the political repercussions, the musical result—through court patronage and competition—was to evenly spread the latest styles across the continent.

As a member of the Swedish Royal Chapel and with the sponsorship of the king, Roman was able to travel extensively. He spent six years in England where he may have studied with Pepusch and known Handel. In his forties, he took a two-year tour of England, France, Italy, Austria, and Germany. Having absorbed the musical idioms of these countries, he was able to compose in all the styles and forms of his day, and he produced vocal works, both secular and sacred; orchestral scores such as suites, sinfonias, overtures and concertos; and chamber music. His chamber music included trio sonatas, landmark *assaggi* for solo violin, and—worthy of special attention by guitarists—twelve harpsichord sonatas.

I have not found a composition date for the *Twelve Sonatas*. Indeed, Roman's music is difficult to date or even attribute, as nearly all his works were unpublished during his lifetime and are known only through his often unsigned manuscripts or hand copies made by others. Stylistically, they fall somewhere between Couperin and J. C. Bach, and they are noteworthy for their rhythmic variety and clarity of structure. Happily for guitarists, the pitch range of the *Sonatas* is a bit narrower than typical in Baroque harpsichord sonatas and suites. I do not know if this is due to the particular instrument for which Roman composed or is just an idiosyncrasy of his methods. Having scrounged through all of these pieces I can heartily recommend them as fruitful source material for transcription.

For this issue's featured transcription, I have chosen the first movement of *Sonata VIII*. Originally in the key of A major, it is marked "commodo" in Italian, meaning "easy" or "comfortable," and so is to be played at moderate speed. The transcription itself was entirely straightforward, requiring only octave transpositions of a few bass notes. The ornaments—short and long trills—can all be accommodated on the guitar and I have arranged the fingerings accordingly. This is material in which you can employ cross-string trills to good effect.

Sonata VIII

Transcribed for guitar
by Richard Yates

Johann Helmich Roman
(1694–1758)

Commodo

98

This page has been left blank to avoid awkward page turns.

Toccata Three

Girolamo Kapsberger

Eight years ago in one of the first articles in this series, I spun a fantasy of discovering a previously unknown manuscript of music by a famous composer, one that had been lost for centuries. In the years since then, my searches have yielded only more recent and better known music that was, for the most part, hidden in plain sight. So I suffered a degree of envy on hearing of a real discovery, just as I had imagined. Happily, envy was soon overtaken by the joy found in the music itself and in the anticipation of being able to carry the discovery, if not to the world, at least to the readers of *Soundboard*.

Girolamo Kapsberger's third collection of music for chitarrone was published in 1626, when he was at the height of his career in the service of the famous Barberini family. He was so esteemed that his masses were performed in the Sistine Chapel that year at the request of Pope Urban VIII. His earlier and later collections of chitarrone music have survived, but the *Libro Terzo* was believed to be lost forever. However, one copy managed to survive those nearly 400 years, and when its existence became known, it was purchased at auction by the Gilmore Library of Yale University in December of 2001. In an unusual decision to further its distribution, the library permitted Italian lutenist Diego Cantalupi to include a computer graphics file of the entire manuscript with his compact disk recording (*Cremona MVC 002-009*). Apparently there is, as of this writing, no modern edition, and my correspondence with the Gilmore Library confirmed that there is no other available facsimile edition of this historic music.

The Instrument

The earliest lutes probably had just four courses, but over the years additional ones were added on the bass end to increase the range until, around 1600, 10-course instruments were common. Kapsberger may well have been a force in further additions—at least his solo music requires more strings than anyone else's. The chitarrone tuning chart in the introduction to *Libro Terzo* shows 19 courses arranged in this pattern. On a solo guitar staff they are transposed up an octave for easier reference:

The courses on the fretboard are doubled

On the fretboard   Off the fretboard

Figure 1, 19-course chitarrone tuning

(paired unison strings); the rest are single. Notice that the large number of strings does not indicate as large a range as one might expect; it can be easily managed on the guitar. However, the overall low pitch does require transposition upwards.

The Notation

A sample from the original, measures 27 through 30, will illustrate other problems faced by the guitarist who wishes to transcribe this music.

Although its location is a bit disorienting, the top five-line staff is a standard bass clef that shows a continuo part. This line rarely uses Baroque figured bass conventions to show inversions, but Kapsberger does include sharp signs to show a major third in a chord and is also careful to write the figures for suspensions. The lower six-line staff is the chitarrone tablature. As is standard with Italian lute tablature, numbers on the lines show which fret to stop. Each line represents one of the six courses on the fretboard. The bottom line represents the courses closest to the floor—what we guitarists would call the first string. Note that this is not the highest pitched string as the third course has that distinction. Strings off the fretboard are shown by symbols above the tablature staff. The seventh string looks like a whole note with one ledger line, as in the last measure of Figure 2. The eighth through 19th strings are shown by numbers. That is a "9" just above the tablature starting the first measure. Note durations are shown by the notes, flags and dots that float above the tablature staff. I chose this example because it is one of the clearest ones. It is a formidable challenge to read faint and overlapping figures and to identify and rectify errors, and

Kapsberger's music is famous for measures that do not add up quite correctly.

The Music

The *Libro Terzo* is noteworthy, not only for its rarity but especially for the quality of the music. While Kapsberger's other solo music is often intriguing and inventive, it sometimes tends to wander rather formlessly. Inspired moments are strung together without much cohesion. And the toccata—the form that comprises the majority of the pieces in this book—is one that, by its nature, is susceptible to this shortcoming. Toccatas are free-form compositions that display technical facility over textural complexity. The description "idiomatic to the keyboard with chords interspersed with running figures and counterpoint" applies equally to toccatas for fretted instruments. The seven toccatas in *Libro Terzo* fit these descriptions, but they each have a clearly shaped character and there is careful attention to the proportions of each section. The impression is one of a tighter, more unified structure. It is intriguing to speculate about the possible influence, or even friendly rivalry, that may have occurred between Kapsberger and another, more famous, composer of toccatas with whom he worked during this period—that other "Girolamo," Frescobaldi.

The Transcription

Aside from the difficult task of decoding the notation, there were several significant decisions in making this guitar transcription. The first concerned the continuo part on the bass staff. In an accompanied Baroque solo piece the continuo line usually indicates how to fill in the harmony, but also serves as the actual bass line of the composition—that is, it has the lowest notes. Another look at Figure 1 shows that this is not so simple in Kapsberger's toccatas. Remember that in Figure 1 the tuning has been transposed up an octave for easier reading and the guitar clef makes an additional octave transposition from a normal treble clef. Sorting through these transpositions and looking now at Figure 2, the first bass note (the "9") in the chitarrone tablature is actually one octave below the E note in the bass line. Surveying the whole score shows that nearly all of the continuo line is simply unison or octave doubling of the lowest chitarrone notes. So it seems that the primary purpose of the continuo here is to help add text—a guide for an additional, optional player—rather than to be an essential structural element. As such, most of it could be ignored in the guitar transcription.

With familiarity, you will find that the music is highly sectional, so much so that the sections are almost like small movements calling for more separation than mere phrases. They also lend themselves to different tempos. Although they are not indicated as such in the original, I have marked these sections with doubled barlines.

One other issue in the transcription became unexpectedly thorny. Kapsberger uses a symbol with two dots separated by a short line—much like our mathematical "divided by" symbol—

to indicate chords that should be arpeggiated. I have carried these into the guitar score. In the introduction he included examples of chords with various numbers of notes and instructions for the order in which the strings should be played in arpeggiating. While this initially seemed helpful, it soon became clear that the difficulties were only beginning. The examples are not exhaustive of the possible chords or even of the actual ones in the score. In some, it seems that the examples are intended to show only the order to pluck the strings so that they sound in ascending order of pitch—remember that the re-entrant tuning complicates things. But other examples are not consistent elsewhere in the score, or to make matters more confusing, his other books. A further question is whether the examples are intended to show ways in which the player might play the chords, that is, suggestions, or whether Kapsberger considered them mandatory. In my naivete, I thought it would be fruitful to investigate further through translation of the Italian text that accompanies the examples. Knowing little Italian, I found a translation service online and hired a professional translator in Italy to work on the passage. After several weeks of stormy miscommunication, and even after consulting a second translator, it became clear that the distinction in meaning that I sought may simply have been lost in 400 years of changes to the language. I will happily leave a firm conclusion on this point to others. Until then, the free nature of the toccata and the fact that we are "translating" between considerably different—albeit fretted—instruments suggest that we can play the arpeggios as we will. After all, historical purists have dismissed us already and Girolamo is not around to disapprove!

Toccata Three

Libro Terzo d'Intavolatura di Chitarrone, 1626

Transcribed for guitar
by Richard Yates

G. G. Kapsberger
(c.1580–1651)

This page has been left blank to avoid awkward page turns.

Pavane

Marin Marais

I have kept in mind, in composing them, the making of them suitable for all sorts of instruments—such as the organ, harpsichord, theorbo, lute violin, German flute—and I dare flatter myself that I have succeeded. —Marin Marais, Preface to *Pieces de Violes, Book II* (1701)

Some transcriptions are serendipitous, as when a random attempt to transcribe an attractive but unlikely score succeeds unexpectedly. Others seem a sure thing from the start. The latter is the case with this installment of *The Transcriber's Art*, especially given the promise in the preface and in the title of piece 116 from that collection, *"Pavane—according to the taste of the former composers for the lute."* Such music should practically transcribe itself. However, although it ultimately works well on the guitar, getting there was not so simple.

Marin Marais (1656–1728) was one of the most prominent musical figures of the French Baroque period. He excelled both as a viol virtuoso and composer, the latter under the training of Jean Baptiste Lully. He is best known for his operas, and especially for his five volumes of viol music published over a span of 39 years. The viols are a family of instruments with only vestigial existence these days, but still extant due to enthusiasts of historically informed performance. At one time viols were more popular than the violin family that supplanted them.

Roughly violin shaped and played with a bow, they differed in that they had frets, flat backs, and six strings tuned in fourths except for a third in the middle—which also describes lutes. While the treble instrument of the violin family is the most prominent, that of the viols was the bass, and it is for this instrument that most solo viol music was written. The pitch of the bass viol was nearly identical to the modern guitar—another tantalizing attraction for transcribers, but one that becomes problematic in the musical context of melody instrument plus continuo.

The combination of a melody instrument plus figured bass accompaniment was endemic to the Baroque era. Most often the solo part was written for an instrument with a higher pitch range than the continuo part—often flute or violin. For guitar transcribers, the general approach is to find a convenient key for the solo part, add the bass line below with judicious octave transpositions as necessary, and fill in some harmony notes in between as indicated by the figures. A quick look at the raw material from a piece for accompanied bass viol immediately shows the problems this combination presents.

Figure 1

In this section the bass line is comprised almost exclusively of a doubling of the viol. Like much Baroque music for solo instrument, this simulates counterpoint by switching between two virtual voices. Obviously, any harmonies based on the figures would sound higher in pitch than the viol. This presents no particular problems for harpsichord accompaniment as the viol's voice is continuous and powerful enough to attract and sustain the listener's attention. In a transcription for solo guitar, however, it is not idiomatic. The solution is to separate the bass and melody, providing more pitch space for the harmony, and then to tease out the real melody from the viol's entwined bass line. Overall, this puts the guitar transcriber in the peculiar position of extracting—from a single line played on two instruments—two or more implied voices, and then having to play them on a single instrument!

Perhaps the most recognizable trait in French Baroque music is its ornamentation. The ostensibly simple harpsichord dances of Couperin or Rameau decorate spare lines with dense flourishes and frills. Although details may vary with each performance or performer, these ornaments are not optional; a guitar transcription must make careful accommodations.

It is fortunate that Marais provided explicit directions in this regard in the introductions to his collections of viol suites. The topic of French Baroque ornamentation is a huge one, far larger than can be addressed here. For the piece under consideration, only three types of ornaments need to be illustrated.

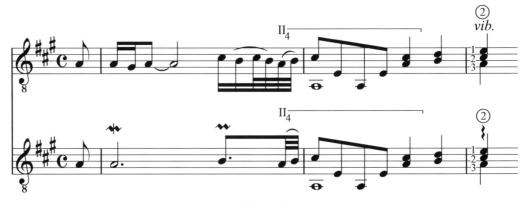

Figure 2

108

Marais was meticulous and accurate in his notation. His scores include a wealth of ornamentation signs, as well as right- and left-hand fingerings, string numbers, and even slides and barrés—all very similar to modern guitar editions, although the symbols are different. He may have been the first to use a circle to indicate an open string.

The first ornament in Figure 2 is a mordent (Marais called it a *batement*). It is a single oscillation between the primary note and the interval of a second below it. According to Gordon Kinney, who edited two volumes of Marais' music for the *Recent Researches in the Music of the Baroque Era* series, the lower note is the diatonic second unless the decorated note is the keynote, or sometimes, the fifth of the triad.

The second ornament—on the B note in Figure 2—is the *tremblement*. Its interpretation is far more complicated. An oscillation with the scale degree above the decorated note, it may be long or short, and start on the main note or on the auxiliary, depending on context. It may be immediate or delayed. I suggest that guitarists try all of these possibilities and select the best fit, musically and technically.

The ornament on the top note of the last chord, a vertical wavy line, is one of two that Marais used to show vibrato. This *plainte* was executed with one left-hand finger. He distinguished this from a *pincé* or *flatement*—a two-fingered vibrato producing, presumably, a larger amplitude, one suitable for longer notes or slower tempos.

I am indebted to Jim Abraham for pointing me to this music. It is clear that there is an abundance of excellent raw material here for guitarists.

In 1995 I responded to a note in *Soundboard* from former editor-in-chief Peter Danner soliciting contributions from readers. One article led to another and it has now, amazingly to me, been ten years since the beginning of *The Transcriber's Art*. Through readers' contributions I have met many enthusiastic and skillful musicians. It has been a marvelous experience and the responses I have received have been a continuing incentive to seek out music that can be adapted for the guitar and shared with readers. While immensely gratifying, there is always more to find.

Pavane

Book II, No. 116

Transcribed for guitar
by Richard Yates

Marin Marais
(1656–1728)

111

Faisant un Bouquet and Sicilienne
Charles Koechlin

Over the years the sources for transcription materials that have appeared in *The Transcriber's Art* have shifted with advances in technology. The first submission I received was a photocopy of a score that I painstakingly duplicated with my preferred scoring program, Finale. With the explosive expansion of the Internet there has been a proportionate increase in the variety of electronic resources. Numerous sites now offer pay-for-download or even free-download scores. I have recently been exploring a particularly cost-effective source of digital scores—those sold as compact disks of graphic files of public domain material under the brand "CD Sheet Music, LLC" (www.cdsheetmusic.com). Please note that I have no financial interest in these products but simply believe that transcribers will find them a treasure trove of material. The compact discs include thousands of pages of Acrobat Reader files of music published before 1925. The two transcriptions that accompany this article were discovered on the French Piano Music disc, which features more than 2,300 pages of music from well-known and not so well-known composers. Each page cost less than a penny!

The Composer

Charles Koechlin (1867–1950), the composer of this issue's featured transcriptions, was intimately associated with the best composers of his time and place. His name recognition has faded over time, but this is due more to the vagaries of history than to any lack of quality in his music, his productivity, or his longevity. He began study at the Paris Conservatoire at age 23 and was a leading figure in the Paris musical scene for more than thirty years. His close associates included Massenet, Ravel, Satie, Debussy, and Fauré. His compositions include settings for the stage, orchestra, chorus, chamber ensembles, solo instruments, and solo voice, as well as—later in life—film scores. His compositional interests ranged from strict counterpoint—stemming from his deep admiration for J. S. Bach—to polytonal works.

The Music

Although Koechlin lived until 1950, most of his compositions for solo piano date from before 1930 and are now within the public domain. The two transcriptions here are from a set of *24 Equisse*—drafts or sketches—composed between 1905 and 1915. Nearly all are within reach of the guitar while retaining melodic grace and harmonic charm. Transcription was uncomplicated, requiring only a few octave transpositions in the bass and an occasional revoiced chord. *En Faisant un Bouquet* ("Making a Bouquet"), is marked *Allegro moderato,* but has a carefree and irregular pattern of short phrases that works well at an easy tempo. The barring is irregular in the original and I have retained that format in the transcription, but it is also a bit puzzling. In most places it seems to mark off phrases, but in others it seems almost arbitrary—for instance, the first phrase in the fifth system. *Sicilienne* has the familiar, gently rocking 6/8 meter but also has irregular and infrequent barring. Here it does not obscure clear phrase boundaries.

En Faisant un Bouquet

Op. 41, No. 7

Transcribed for guitar
by Richard Yates

Charles Koechlin
(1867–1950)

Sicilienne

Op. 41, No. 10

Transcribed for guitar
by Richard Yates

Charles Koechlin
(1867–1950)

Calme

This page has been left blank to avoid awkward page turns.

Largo
Richard Jones

In delving through the history of music for pieces to present in this column, my searches have often led away from famous composers, as generations of guitarists have already rummaged through their works for every possible transcription. I have found success, and often great pleasure, in discovering—or rather, rediscovering—the obscure or forgotten composers. The risk of readers passing by an unrecognized name at the head of this page with the brief thought "Who? Never heard of him" is balanced by those, such as yourself, who pause to investigate and find something new and delightful.

Music history undoubtedly favors the preservation of the music of composers with substantial output; the sheer number of pages produced is some insurance against the erosion of time. And of course, those who produced a large body of work have usually done so because they knew a thing or two about music. But the converse is not always true. This issue's composer certainly fits that pattern: Obscure now, he was possibly obscure even in his own time, and had only a slim portfolio. The quality, however, is quite remarkable, as you will see.

The Composer

Richard Jones' birth date is unknown, but he first appears in history about 1730 when he became director of the playhouse orchestra at Drury Lane Theatre Royale in London. This theater was a cultural center for several hundred years but seems to have been used mostly for plays rather than musical performances. Jones composed shows including a masque, a pantomime, and a ballad opera. His other works are limited to a song or two, airs and suites for violin, and *Six Suits or Setts of Lessons* for the harpsichord or spinet.

The Music

The *Six Suites* contain most of the standard dance movements we associate with High Baroque suites, along with many extra ones, often in a different order than we are used to. Indeed, the sixth suite has twelve movements in four different keys and seems more a collection than a suite. The fourth suite, from which this column's example is drawn, follows more closely the usual template: *Prelude* (titled *Largo*), *Allemanda*, *Sarabanda*, *Minuet*, *Giga*, and *Borée*. All of the movements work well on the guitar with minimal adaptation. Most notable throughout Jones' music is the violinistic character of the melodies. Rapid runs, wide leaps, florid ornamentation, and *bariolages* suffuse the music. We know that Jones was himself a violinist because he had pupils who became well-known, and so it seems plausible that he composed using the violin and then adapted the score to the keyboard. We would do well to keep this in mind as it has implications for both transcription and performance.

The Transcription

No unusual techniques were necessary to produce the guitar transcription. The wide range and occasional large leaps of the melody sometimes made it difficult to avoid crossing the bass or interior lines but these challenges were, in all cases, relatively easy to resolve.

One aspect of the transcription does warrant discussion, though, and is a good illustration of how fingering must be informed by musical considerations. The *Largo*, with its stately tempo, numerous ornaments, and dotted rhythms throughout, is entirely in the French tradition. Although Jones was English, he composed during a period in which regional styles had been thoroughly integrated across national boundaries. He worked in London when that prominent cultural center had recently surpassed Paris to become the largest city in Europe, and certainly was conversant with the latest and most popular styles and techniques. The notation of dotted rhythms in this period was only approximate, unlike today's precise definitions. Double dotting had yet to appear consistently in music notation. So in French style a dotted rhythm, as in the combination of dotted eighth plus sixteenth, apparently meant something closer to what we would write as double-dotted eighth plus thirty-second. Actually, in this style it is almost impossible to make the short notes too short. I recommend practicing such pieces with exaggerated dotting as that will quickly reveal those places that need more attention. Consider the following example to show how this can affect fingering decisions.

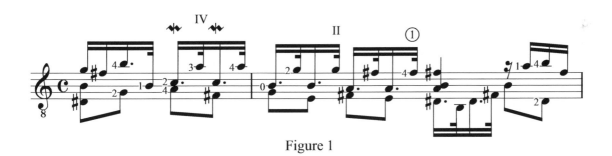

Figure 1

In Figure 1, notice the timing of the placement of the barrés at the fourth fret and then at the second fret. We are trained to think of the quarter note as the unit of beat, which it is, but our thinking about fingering and shifting should not blindly follow these unit divisions. In a heavily dotted rhythm with very short notes preceding the downbeat, the units of fingering are shifted. In the example, a naive player might protest that placing the barré at the short note cuts off the bass note from its full duration. But this consideration is far less important than maintaining the sharp, snappy character of the melody. In fact, cutting the bass note a bit short allows the short melody note to sound through more clearly. A bonus is that this fingering is far easier than shifting, barring or placing left-hand fingers right after the short note: With the left hand positioned and the fingers placed on the short note and the notes that immediately follow, all attention can be on quick execution by the right hand. You will find many places in the *Largo* where fingering this way will lessen the difficulties and facilitate the fine control of timing that is essential to expression of this music.

Largo

Suite IV, Lessons for the Harpsichord or Spinnet
(1732)

Transcribed for guitar
by Richard Yates

Richard Jones
(?–1744)

La Forqueray

Jacques Duphly

In the year 1742 a young musician made his way through the French countryside toward the center of the cultural universe—Paris. He had been born in the last year of the reign of the Sun King, Louis XIV, whose court was the epitome of extravagance and opulence, and after an early career as an organist in obscure provincial towns, decided to try his luck in the big city. He was known for his gentle and inoffensive manner and a musical style similar to Rameau's. His playing and music were described by D'Aquin: "He has a lightness of touch and a certain softness which, sustained by ornaments, marvelously render the character of his pieces."

At that same time, another momentous event in a musical life occurred. A bass viol virtuoso advanced to Musicien du Chambre du Roy, a prominent and profitable position that had been held by his father for more than 40 years. The story of the father and son is one of dysfunction and intrigue, with the father described as bad-tempered, temperamental, self-important, and unpleasant. The boy's mother had served as harpsichord accompanist for the father until she abandoned him, when the son was eleven. Possibly out of jealousy or paranoia, the father once had his son thrown into prison and later temporarily exiled.

Thus, the lives of the two musicians—the provincial keyboard player and composer, Jacques Duphly, and the cosmopolitan bass viol virtuoso, Jean-Baptiste Forqueray—intersected. It is not known if they ever performed together, but they would certainly have known each other

through their musical activities. Duphly became part of the inner circle of professional and aristocratic connoisseurs—essentially the royal court. Forqueray published his father's compositions for viol, with freely arranged versions for harpsichord, shortly after the father died. And Duphly published four volumes of harpsichord music including, in the third book of 1756, a piece titled, simply, *La Forqueray.*

The Music

La Forqueray is in the form of a rondeau, in which a refrain alternates with several episodes or, as labeled by Duphly, "couplets." Rondeaux were a favorite of Duphly and they constitute a larger portion of his music than any other form. He experimented with different proportions throughout the four volumes of his published works. *La Forqueray* has a refrain with an entirely symmetrical and regular sixteen bars comprised of two eight-bar periods, each containing two four-bar phrases. However, the three couplets deviate from the usual rondeau format in that each couplet is longer than the previous one.

Originally in the rather remote key of F minor, *La Forqueray* clearly aims to emulate the music of the bass viol. The music is confined almost entirely to two bass clefs and rises no higher than the D natural note found on the first string of the guitar. The third couplet employs the *style brisé* in which broken, arpeggiated chords imply a contrapuntal texture. Originally borrowed from lute music, it was quite common in Baroque keyboard music. Perhaps the use of it in *La Forqueray* was meant to suggest, not the lute, but rather, the virtuosic viol technique of the player for whom the piece is titled. One can imagine that the difficulties of manipulating a viol bow in this way would have been considerable.

The Transcription

Because of the limited pitch range and a texture suitable for viol, only small changes were needed to adapt the music to the guitar. Unusual in transcriptions of music from keyboard to guitar, the pitch was actually raised a minor third to the key of A minor. But particular attention was required for the fingering to preserve the numerous *agréments*, or ornaments, that are essential to this style. Trills, mordents, and appoggiaturas are sprinkled liberally throughout. The following figure shows examples of how these might be played.

Figure 1

The third couplet posed a transcription puzzle in that the note durations could not be easily sustained throughout. The keyboard notation, if it were on one staff, would look like this.

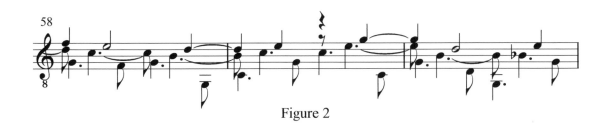

Figure 2

While many of these overlapping, suspended voice movements could be played on the guitar, many others could not. To attempt to show them in a literal fashion would have been both arduous for the engraver and cluttered for the player. The solution is to think back to the origin of this keyboard style—the lute. The keyboard notation is itself just a way of suggesting the over-ringing of notes that is an idiosyncratic feature of the lute (and guitar) sound, so a slavish adherence to the letter of the keyboard notation would be misplaced. The most judicious means of notating this section seems to be to reduce the notation to two voices by preserving the bass line, which is actually the more prominent voice, while combining the two upper lines. As a reminder that the over-ringing is to be allowed where convenient, I have added laissez vibrer ties. While I generally avoid these in my transcriptions, they seemed apt, and possibly instructive, in this instance. Fingering has been carefully selected to facilitate their execution.

La Forqueray

Pièces de Clavecin, Livre III, 1756

Transcribed for guitar
by Richard Yates

Jacques Duphly
(1715–1789)

Andantino

George Onslow

When guitarists approach the transcribed music of an unfamiliar composer, it can be useful to see where he fits in the historical context with which guitarists are already familiar. Getting our bearings within the pantheon of guitar composers can give a start to answering the questions of interpretation and performance practice necessary for a thorough understanding of the music and its effective communication. For the composer in this installment of *The Transcriber's Art*, the birth and death dates and a little geography are sufficient.

George Onslow was born in 1784 in France (although his father was English—note that his first name is spelled George, not Georges). Onslow traveled extensively and studied piano across the continent, but France remained his musical center. He resisted, to a degree, the inevitable attraction that living in Paris had for musicians of his era, but did spend winter months there to arrange for the performance and publication of his compositions. As a composer, he was ranked with the best of his time.

The whims of history distort the eminence with which we perceive composers from centuries past, even to the extent that sometimes the most highly esteemed become all but forgotten. Onslow was compared favorably with Mozart, Schubert, and Mendelssohn and was known as "the French Beethoven." His decline from historical prominence may be, in part, because his musical output was limited, although it was considerably varied: stage works, three operas, four symphonies, miscellaneous chamber works

with piano and—perhaps the best known and most sophisticated—34 string quartets and 37 string quintets.

To evoke the musical zeitgeist in which he wrote, consider the composers and performers that made Paris the center of the guitar universe at the time. Ferdinando Carulli was an Italian but settled in Paris about 1808. Others followed, including Matteo Carcassi (just eight years younger than Onslow), Dionisio Aguado, and Fernando Sor. One might wonder if Sor, "the Beethoven of the Guitar," and Onslow ever met and compared nicknames.

The Music

The *Six Pièces pour Piano* were composed about 1848, very late in Onslow's career. In fact, it had been nearly 30 years since he had composed solo piano music. While no information has survived about the circumstances that prompted the music, guitarists can be grateful that it has descended to our day. The six all have the qualities that suggest good potential for transcription, including a melodic and harmonic charm, and an economy of scale. The one that I have chosen is the longest and most complex of the set.

Andantino molto espressivo is episodic and dramatic, possibly recalling the composer's experience with opera. There is frequent chromaticism —characteristic of Onslow—and ample opportunities for the intimate expressiveness that works so well on the guitar.

The Transcription

Transposing just one step down from E major to D major allowed the range of the original to be retained, with only a few notes in the bass requiring octave transposition. This transposition also placed the pedal points—found in several sections—conveniently on the open sixth, fifth and fourth strings. In fact, were it not for this circumstance, the piece would have been quite difficult, if not impossible, to play on the guitar. For instance, in the section beginning at measure 54, the open A allows the high three-note chords to be played without compromising the tessitura of the original. These chords are notated in a manner that may not be entirely familiar to guitarists. A treble *8va* marking has been used to show that the chords (but not the bass notes) are to be played an octave higher. Through measure 57, these all fall neatly onto the first three strings in quite manageable configurations. In measures 58–59 a compromise was necessary; the middle notes of the chords have been lowered an octave. This is a good piece for learning to be more comfortable negotiating the upper reaches of the fretboard.

One caution about navigation should be made: At measure 44 a second ending appears. This is the final measure of the piece. The first time you play through this spot, jump over measure 44 to measure 45, which is marked as a first ending. This somewhat unusual layout seemed the least cluttered and also conserved valuable space.

The second beat of measure 35 might be awkward but becomes easier if you place the third finger on the F natural first, just after the B flat is played. This cuts the E flat note a little short but is hardly noticeable. Then, with the third finger firmly placed, the second and fourth finger find their notes easily.

The barré on the tenth fret at measure 48 is less difficult if the fourth finger is used as a guide finger from the previous A note.

In measure 50, hitting the chord topped by an E natural is greatly simplified by recognizing that the third finger stays in place on the A note. Again, move out of that chord, as in measure 48, by using the fourth finger as a guide.

Six Pièces pour Piano

VI

Transcribed for guitar
by Richard Yates

George Onslow
(1784–1853)

Andantino molto espressivo

Je te veux

Erik Satie

In researching music for this series of articles I have often looked for obscure composers or previously untranscribed pieces by well-known composers. Regular readers have seen the music of 33 different composers, with only Bach, Chopin and Kapsberger having multiple appearances. The composer of this issue's featured transcription is not only well-known but may have actually written the music most frequently transcribed and played on the guitar. Has any beginning guitarist not played one or more of Erik Satie's *Gymnopédies*? And have not most of us taken our own stab at transcribing them from the piano score? The *Gymnopédies* work well on the guitar because they are short, of reasonable range, thin in texture, moderate in tempo, and beautiful in effect. It is a small step from these to the three *Gnossiennes*, although they do add a bit of difficulty. And similarly, beyond those we find … what? Well, almost nothing. A large and apparently unexamined source of transcription material lies waiting.

The Composer

Erik Satie (1866–1925) wrote music that spanned the gap from eminently popular waltz-songs of the Parisian cabaret to the most abstract and radical anticipations of music of the 20th century. Debussy recognized his music as the forerunner of Impressionism, and his experiments in minimalism anticipated John Cage and even Philip Glass. Satie strove for clarity, brevity, simplicity and precision. As is often true of artistic revolutionaries, his most elevated art

could not support him and so he made a living as an accompanist in the cafés of Paris and as a composer and conductor of theatrical entertainments.

Je te veux

Satie's precarious financial state required him to pitch new songs to singers who might add them to their repertoires. Paulette Darty was a music-hall star billed as the "Queen of the Slow Waltz." A striking and statuesque presence, she would waltz around the stage between verses and songs. In her account of their first meeting she wrote: "Usually I received composers in the morning when they came to present their new tunes to me. That morning, my secretary admitted Erik Satie, whose name was then completely unknown to me … That morning I was in my bath. I heard the now-famous tune of *Je te veux* … which had such a special charm and such an attractive quality about it. I quickly got out of my bath to express my enchantment personally."

Mademoiselle Darty sang it frequently in recitals and shows and it became Satie's best known and most lucrative composition. While the piece was originally a song, Satie soon made a piano solo version that included additional material and was published in 1904.

Transcription

The ease with which *Je te veux* translates to the guitar adds to my surprise that it has not been done before (I was able to find only an abridged version in a web search of music publishers). Indeed, it required little more than the usual transformations commonly used for this type of keyboard texture: Octave doublings in the melody and bass were reduced to single notes and a few accompaniment chords were inverted. Only once did the harmony need to be simplified slightly to accommodate the guitar.

Figure 1

Choosing a key worked out very nicely. The original has sections in four different keys: C major, G major, F major, and B flat major. This variety portended difficulties for a convenient transcription, although the four keys lie in a tidy cluster adjacent to each other in the circle of fifths. It was simply fortuitous that transposition up a few steps in the circle—to A major, E major, D major, and G major—placed the music within the most congenial harmonic region for the guitar while setting the highest parts of the melody in hospitable territory on the fretboard.

Performance

As with any waltz with this texture, the melody must sing through clearly. As Satie wrote: "Do not forget that the melody is the Idea, the outline; as much as it is the form and the subject matter of the work. The harmony is an illumination, an exhibition of the object, its reflection." Note that the melody is often not on the top but, rather, in the middle or bass voice. The section starting at bar 119 warrants special attention in this regard, especially because the melody is syncopated. In this circumstance, a very light touch with the high accompaniment works best.

One caution about this particular transcription is in order. To contain the piece within the three pages that sit easily on a music stand, it was necessary to use an unusual layout of repeats. The first repeat—bar 117 jumping back to bar 102—is clear enough, but the second ending goes all the way to bar 150 before jumping back to bar 102. Then, and here it gets ugly, the third ending, at bar 151, is only one bar long and requires you to go back to the *Segno* at bar 6. From there, play straight through to bar 68 at the bottom of the first page and then on to the *Coda* on page three. Once you clearly understand the map, you will be able to dispense with the score and waltz about the stage as you perform.

Je te veux

Transcribed for guitar
by Richard Yates

Erik Satie
(1866–1925)

134

135

Nocturne, Op. 15, No. 3

Frédéric Chopin

As a classical guitarist, my focus is on transcription rather than arrangement. The distinction between these terms varies with time, genre and geography, but there is some agreement that transcription aims to transfer music without alteration from one instrument to another, while arrangement takes only selected elements—the melody, for instance—and deliberately introduces new material or transformations of the old. Although this definition of transcription seems well defined, in actual practice things are much more complicated. Even if every note is transferred intact from, say, a piano piece, there are many other aspects and qualities of the music that are inevitably affected. Transcribers must carefully evaluate these possibilities and make thoughtful decisions about what to preserve and what to modify, and while an arranger's personal musical expression is more explicitly evident, the transcriber's musical values and aesthetic sensibilities are no less involved in the process or evident in the finished piece.

As I work on a transcription, my goal—only rarely reached in practice—is to maintain fidelity to the original by preserving those aspects I consider to be essential, and at the same time, to produce a score that looks, sounds, and feels as if it were originally written on and for the guitar. This process, if done conscientiously, is painstaking. You will quickly see that the minutiae in this article contrast with earlier ones, and my fear is that this will divert readers from sharing in my rediscovery of this transcription. However, if you persevere you may find insights that are useful in your personal involvement with our marvelous instrument, whether you are performing, writing, arranging, transcribing, or even simply listening.

I first made this transcription several years ago for my collection, *Chopin for Acoustic Guitar*, published by Mel Bay Publications. Although at first reluctant to revisit old territory, I soon found it fascinating to retrace my steps in light of the transcription work I have done since that time.

The music is the *Nocturne, Op. 15, No. 3*, by Frédéric Chopin, originally composed for piano solo. Chopin's music is universally recognized as some of the most original and profound in history. It presents daunting transcription challenges for several reasons. His piano pieces are monuments of the composer's art that demand respect, inspire awe, and immediately reveal incompetent handling. They are also intimately wedded, both in our culture and in the details of their construction and technique, to a specific instrument—the piano. Thus, it has been thoroughly gratifying to discover Chopin pieces that survive aesthetically and even reveal new facets in translation to the guitar.

I will discuss the music sequentially, explaining the puzzles, options and solutions that I chose. In reading this, it may sound like transcription is an entirely orderly and rational process. The reality is much more chaotic, as decisions affect each other and sometimes several problems must be solved simultaneously. There is also more trial and error than may be evident from this account, and some solutions are, despite post hoc rationalizations, simply what seem to sound best. Finally, absent from this account are the many pieces that were simply abandoned when I was unable to find adequate solutions.

Notation

Fingerings and other decisions that are embodied in this score are all, in a sense, only suggestions. Guitarists are notorious for overlooking, ignoring, and changing fingerings. The ones that I selected here were evaluated in close detail, as you will see, and I suggest that the player may benefit from carefully considering the rationale for their selection and make changes only after analyzing the possibilities. Remember that fingering on the guitar, with its polyphonic capabilities on a two-dimensional grid, is a complex subject, and many of the best solutions are not the most obvious ones. I have assumed that the reader is familiar with the most common conventions used in classical guitar scores. Briefly, small numbers in front of note heads refer to left-hand fingers, Roman numerals show barré positions—they are sometimes accompanied by small Arabic numerals to show the number of barréd strings—and circled numbers indicate a specific string to use for a note.

For easier reference, I have paired the original piano score with the guitar transcription. However, I have made some modifications to facilitate comparisons. First, the piano score, originally in the key of G minor, is presented in the transposed key (D minor), in order to save the reader the trouble of mentally transposing. But doing this meant moving some notes from the bass to the treble clef and using more leger lines for bass notes than would be standard piano score practice. You will see that treble clef notes in the piano score go down to the low D as in the guitar version. Although there is some risk of confusion through mid-measure clef changes, my intent was to make the piano score as readable as possible for guitarists.

Key Selection

The first choices are always those keys that sit best on the guitar and this list is rather short. In the major mode we have G, D, and A, and sometimes F, C, and E; in the minor mode, D, A, and E, (only rarely G and B). Next, we look at the range of the melody. The contour of the top line is an essential feature that is usually much less amenable to octave changes than is the bass line. If no key can accommodate the top line, as is often the case with piano music, then a workable guitar transcription may not be possible.

Trial and error shows that D minor fits reasonably well for the first 72 measures. It places much of the melody in the range of the guitar that sings well. On the low end, it does not require that the melody drop below the third string G. In D minor, we can see that there are frequent and repeating notes on both A and D, as expected. If necessary, the sixth string can be dropped to accommodate a low D. "Dropped D" tuning allows the use of an open string for this low tonic note. Just as important, a dropped D can often reduce the size of stretches between the bass and melody notes, sometimes bridging the difference between what is impossible and what is possible, and often making what is difficult, easy. Transcription of music from piano to guitar often involves wrestling with the narrower range of the guitar, and dropped D tuning can help tremendously.

Measure 1

As we examine the first measure we see that it is playable as it stands.

137

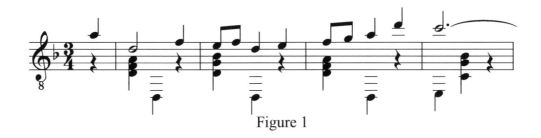

Figure 1

However, the fingering of the chord is difficult in measure 1, very easy in measure 2, and impossible in measures 3 and 4. So, from the outset we are faced with a fundamental problem of transcription. Inevitably, some aspects of the original will be changed. The task is to evaluate and choose which aspects to alter so that others may remain. If we follow a superficial attachment to all of the notes then the project is doomed. And if the back-up plan is simply to play as many of them as possible the result will be merely poor. Finding aesthetically pleasing solutions requires analyzing the components of the composition, weighing their importance and the effects of changes, and ultimately reassembling the music from modified parts. In doing this we must seek and follow some of the creative pathways mapped by the composer. But blindly following that exact path and detouring awkwardly around the obstacles as they are encountered is short-sighted and, ultimately, less satisfying than finding a new trail that closely parallels the original while avoiding barriers that disrupt a smooth course. Transcription is more than just preserving notes; we must consider proportion, pattern, balance, and effect. Beyond this, we must factor in the practical factors such

as playability, difficulty level, stretches, and tempo.

With this in mind, how will we play measure 1? The ideal solution will recognize that there is a pattern to the bass part that continues for the first 76 measures. This pattern is an essential and prominent feature of the piece. A superficial treatment that grabs some notes here and fewer there as dictated by the physical idiosyncrasies of the guitar will lose this essential feature. A much better, and sensitive, plan is to scale down the bass part to a size that can be consistently maintained. We saw almost immediately that three-note chords in the bass on the first beat will not be possible to maintain. A score that reduces these to two notes (in addition to the melody) can be played, but the next challenge is to do this in a way that has the least impact on another essential aspect of the music—the harmony. Theory gives us some guidelines for cutting notes from chords: Delete unisons and octaves, delete the fifths of the chord, do not freely substitute different inversions of the original harmony, etc. These guidelines do not give us answers to altering the bass but, rather, starting points to consider. Applying them to the first three measures gives us this solution.

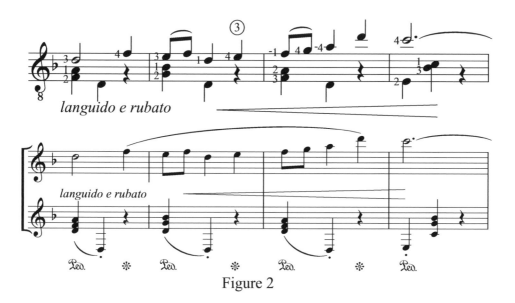

Figure 2

Notice first that the low D on the second beat has been moved up an octave closer to the melody line. This places it in a range where its stepwise intervals can be maintained, for instance, from the D up to the E in measure 4. This is the most common alteration that is made in guitar transcriptions of keyboard music, but the compression of the pitch range in this way has other implications that must be considered, both in transcription and in performance. First, as a practical matter, with less distance between the bass line and the melody there is simply less space for other notes. Second, the close-set texture makes it more difficult to distinguish the melody from the harmony. Thus the accompaniment requires a thinner texture. For performance, the player must pay close attention to dynamically separating the melody from the accompaniment or clarity is at risk. One last observation on this point is a reminder that the pitch of the guitar is a full octave lower than usually shown in scores. So the low D in the bass, moved an octave closer to the melody, is actually now at its original pitch. Overall, the guitar is pitched quite low compared to most melody instruments. One of the consequences is the higher risk of muddiness in the texture—another reason for thinning it.

The solution in Figure 2 also preserves all essential harmony notes in each measure. The potential drawback is that, with the D note deleted from the harmony, the first chord in measure 2 becomes more ambiguous than in the original, where the underlying harmony is a second-inversion G minor triad with non-harmonic tones in the melody. A similar situation occurs at the start of measure 3 where the harmony might be heard as F major rather than D minor. Far outweighing this risk are several factors: First, the recurring D in the bass quickly erases any ambiguity in these, and subsequent, measures. Also, the melody has firmly established itself in the key of D minor and any ambiguities are thus resolved in favor of that key. Third, the harmonic rhythm clearly moves in units of a whole measure.

A last issue that supports the texture chosen for the transcription involves large scale features of the music. While this is a nocturne, it is unlike any others that Chopin wrote. Its triple rhythm, repeated bass notes, accent pattern, and remote harmonic exploration all suggest a slow mazurka. Now, mazurkas, of which Chopin wrote more than 50, are often characterized by accents on the second beats of measures. So, slightly ambiguous chords on the first beat of some measures, rather than detracting from the transcription, actually strengthen it by reinforcing an essential feature: accented second beats.

Measure 2

The fingering that I chose for measure 2 needs explanation. The last note, E, is placed on the third string instead of the (most natural) open first string or the (also logical) second string. I rejected the first string because, although the open string allows easier shifting up the neck,

it is difficult, especially in a slow tempo, to integrate an open string smoothly into a connected, legato melody. It usually sticks out in its volume, timbre and duration. Open strings can be a necessary, even characteristic, fingering resource but they are not without liabilities. They can ease one difficulty but, at the same time, create other obstacles to performance.

Using the second string for this note was a plausible alternative, as you can see in Figure 3a.

Figure 3a

Figure 3b (score)

In its favor is the smooth connection with the preceding D and the consistency of timbre as the melody follows the string all the way to the A. What decided the case in favor of the third string was the left-hand shift that must be made. In Figure 3a, the shift is between the third beat of measure 2 and the first beat of measure 3 rather than a beat earlier. The shift is the same size in both cases—third "position" to sixth (and notice that the index finger can be used as a guide finger in either case). However, in 3a the shift is immediately followed by eighth note motion while in 3b this is delayed one beat. This small difference makes the 3b shift slightly more secure. Also, even if this shift is made quickly, there is a small but inevitable break in the flow of the melody. In my view, it is more important, especially in triple time, to connect the last beat of the measure to the first beat of the next than to connect beat 2 to beat 3. Here again is a very small, perhaps even insignificant, difference. But these small differences and the weights that the transcriber attaches to them accumulate throughout a score and can ultimately

determine whether the result is successful or not.

The open D in the bass also played an interesting, if minor, part in deciding on the fingering in Figure 3b, but explaining its role requires a short digression about the piano. Pianos are all equipped with a sustain pedal that allows notes to continue to sound even after the key has been released. The signs '𝄢' and '✻' under the bass staff instruct the performer to depress and release this pedal, respectively. For other musicians, the use of the sustain pedal can be mysterious and arcane because the notation sometimes appears to be contradictory. An example of these puzzles appears in the first measure. The low D has a staccato mark. This indicates that the note is to be shorter than its written duration by about half. On the other hand, the pedal signs direct depressing the pedal on the first beat and holding it down until the third beat. Without the articulation (Figure 4a) or without the pedal signs (Figure 4b) the transcribed measure would look like this.

140

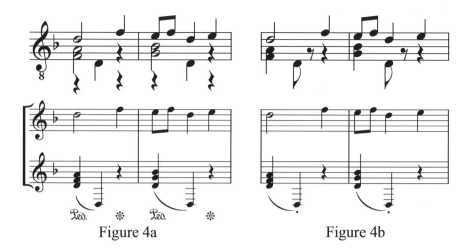

Figure 4a   Figure 4b

Including both the articulation and pedal sign is contradictory because quickly releasing the key for the D note should have no audible effect if the pedal is down. I have been unable to resolve this puzzle in Chopin's music, even after discussing it with well-trained pianists. Some claim an audible difference but cannot explain the physical mechanism that would produce it. Others say that the effect is only a psychological one in the performer. Now, before we guitarists begin to feel superior about our notation in this regard, we need to recognize that we have as much, or more, ambiguity in our scores, particularly about the duration of bass notes. It is common for beginners to allow bass notes to sound too long, but it is also true that scores are not always clear in this regard. Incidentally, much early guitar music, including that written at the time of the *Nocturne*, was no more specific than tablature as to the duration of notes. While the notation of guitar music has improved since that time, note durations in scores are still not always exact prescriptions for performance. The most precise notation for how I understand the music to sound on guitar, although with perhaps some shortening of the low bass note, is shown in Figure 4a. Thankfully, this level of precision is not necessary. Any score is a compromise between precise specifications on one hand and reliance on the player's knowledge and musical

sensibility on the other. Thus, all scores are only guides for performance and can never be exact prescriptions. Those composers who are more finicky about notation are the ones who have most often ignored that notation. This is amply evident after listening to even a small sample of the best performers.

This lengthy digression will have application later on in this analysis but, for now, it brings us back to my last reason for placing the left-hand shift in measure 2, and the reason is also, perhaps, largely psychological. The second beat bass note, D, must be actively stopped from sounding through the third beat because it is an open string. In both the 3a and 3b versions this would be done with the right-hand thumb, but to me it just seems more natural to do this in the course of a left-hand shift, as happens in 3b.

Measure 4

In keeping with the plan to use two-note chords on the second beat, one note must be deleted from the original chord. Certainly the B flat, the seventh of the chord, is essential, but leaving out the G can render an easily fingered chord.

The sustain pedal puzzle deepens, however. The pedal is to be held down until measure 6, yet there are rests in the bass line. My inclination is to ignore the rests and allow notes to ring as shown by the pedal signs. This makes a pleasing contrast to the restraint in the preceding measures.

Measures 7–13

The A note on the last beat and most of the melody for the next seven measures are on the second string. Although the passage is perfectly playable in a lower position, this choice was made because of the musical character of the melody. The repeated descents from the A are sweet, sighing figures that call for vibrato and very slight glissandi between the notes. These are more easily produced in the higher position. This placement of the notes also supports the consistent cutting off of the bass F notes on the third beats.

Measure 8

Harmonic considerations again arise in our plan to reduce the size of the first-beat chords. The chord is a diminished seventh chord, also called an incomplete dominant ninth, which resolves to the temporary tonic, F major. The diminished seventh is unique in that each of its four voices carries equal weight and so each can equally be omitted from the chord without changing its character. We can therefore decide based on the voice leading into the next measure and on practical fingering considerations.

The C half note that ties over and then recurs in measure 10 is more problematic. I have found no reasonable way to include it in the guitar score without greatly disrupting other essential features. As the fifth of the F major chord, it can be omitted without damage to the harmony, and it conveniently appears in the melody that begins in the next measure.

Measure 11

The C note, discussed in the previous section, can be included here. This makes a smoother inflection to the C sharp in the following measure.

Measure 19

The texture thickens briefly to a three-note bass chord. There are a couple of plausible alternatives that keep the two-note texture.

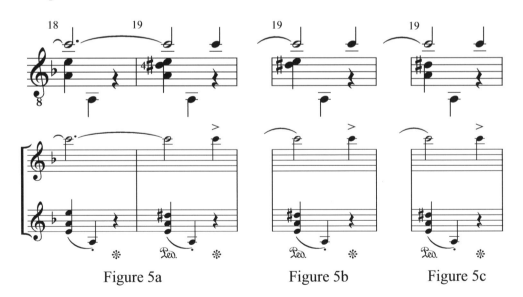

Figure 5a   Figure 5b   Figure 5c

The chord does not yield easily to harmonic analysis. In this context it would be farfetched to call it a ninth chord. Its function seems to be, more simply, a repetition of the chord in the previous measure with the added augmented fourth (D sharp). Of the three notes—A, D sharp, and E—the D sharp must certainly be retained, as it is the only note that distinguishes the chord from the one in the previous measure. It also adds the essential dissonance to the harmony. Omitting the A, as in Figure 5b, is not a good solution because it does not show the similarity with the previous measure. Last, in Figure 5c, omitting the E is logical, and including it adjacent to the D sharp makes a nice biting dissonance. All three of these possibilities are entirely reasonable and the distinctions among them are small. I included them in this discussion because they were actual alternatives that I considered and illustrate the type of considerations that must be weighed. Including all three, as I have in the score (Figure 5a), gives the player the option to choose.

Measure 24

The third, the E note in this dominant seventh chord, can be omitted because the fifth (G) and seventh (B flat) are present.

Measures 51–70

This measure begins a remarkable section of music. The comfortable mood of the first 50 measures first drifts to other keys. Then, the gentle rocking motion becomes increasingly agitated. Eventually, the familiar harmonies are left behind in a dizzying spiral through remote and discordant regions.

Although the harmony becomes more remote from the original key, the same general plan for transcribing the bass can be followed. The low notes on the second beat of every measure allow inversion of the first beat chords without distorting the harmony.

Chopin was a visionary in this fascinating period of Western musical history, during which the harmonic vocabulary was consciously expanded to provide new vistas for musical expression. In large part, the expansion was created by placing increasingly tall and precarious stacks of notes on top of the chords established in the Baroque and Classical periods. Broadly, this meant more different notes in chords—a serious challenge for guitarists. Faced with such challenges, guitar composers struggled mightily to innovate. A few succeeded, but most simply turned away. The reasons can only be speculated. Contributing factors probably included the limits of the instrument, of playing technique, and, sadly, of imagination. Happily, for modern transcribers, this left a gap in the repertoire and a large body of music just waiting to be adapted to the guitar. It gives us an opportunity to demonstrate for the current era what is possible in guitar music.

Measures 56–57

The accompaniment can thin to one note because the melody moves in eighths to fill in the sound. While not completely necessary, this also serves to foreshadow the treatment used in measures 64–76.

Measure 63

The E sharp melody note is tied into this measure but clearly cannot be sustained, as shown, with the 2 finger, which moves to the third string for the C sharp. This apparent contradiction is due to my preferred manner of notating such situations. The meaning I intend to convey is this: The melody is tied over in the original piano score, but on the guitar cannot be held for its written duration without sacrificing some other essential feature. The fingering number shows what to actually do. Preserving the note's duration in the score shows the original form of the line and allows the player to use this information to find other solutions to the problem if desired. Shortening such notes in the score and adding a lot of rests can create a great deal of clutter. Guitar scores already pack more ink into a smaller space than the music for any other instrument and so clarity is to be valued. This procedure may be the guitar's equivalent of the piano's puzzling combination of pedal signs, rests and articulations. In any event, the principle that musical scores can never prescribe all details is reaffirmed.

Measure 64–76

Beginning here, the first beat bass chords are all reduced to one note. This is necessary to minimize the difficulty and make the texture consistent. As before, voice leading, consistency of texture, and management of the difficulty level take priority over the completeness of the harmony. So, to illustrate this with two measures from this section, please consider the next figure.

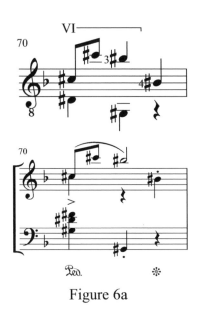

Figure 6a

Figure 6b

In measure 70, Figure 6a, the four treble staff notes are inviolate. Altering their pitches would change the fundamental character of the line. Notice, however, that these four notes constitute two voices in the original that can reasonably be combined into one line in the guitar score. The acoustic difference is very slight, and most players will not dampen the first note until the second quarter beat anyway. Here, I would confidently rely on the player's discretion. The next consideration in this measure is the bass line. The low G sharp bass note throughout this passage, a repeated pedal point, is also essential in my view and will ultimately become magically transformed in measure 88. This leaves the first

beat chord to mull over. It can be interpreted as a G sharp dominant seventh chord. The C sharp notes are non-harmonic tones that resolve to B sharp. Which of the harmonic tones is to be retained? Let's consider them one at a time. The G sharp can go—it is prominent in the bass in this and preceding measures. Next, the F sharp can be dropped because retaining it without one of the other notes of the chord produces a bare, perfect fifth without the dominant dissonant quality. This leaves us with the D sharp. Although it is the fifth of the harmony, and hence in most circumstances a likely candidate for omission, here it provides the piquant dissonance with the C sharp melody note. Further confirmation

144

of this choice comes from examining the voice leading of this and the adjacent measures. The corresponding note in the preceding measure is a C double sharp, while that following is an E sharp. The chosen D sharp fits perfectly in this stepwise sequence.

In measure 76, the rending of the harmonic fabric reaches its peak and the first beat chord has grown to five notes. While the harmony on the first beat is another diminished seventh chord, what can rational analysis make of the second beat and the measure as a whole? The sensible course is to follow through with the pattern of the transcription that has been established. The result, shown in Figure 6b, is what amounts to an atonal cluster of G sharp, A sharp, B sharp and C sharp smeared across the measure that sets the stage for the gradual reconstitution of tonality in the distant key of G sharp major. Guitarists might want to pause here and look around a bit. A key signature for this far-flung realm would have six sharps and one double sharp! You may never visit this key again in your lifetime, but arriving here puts to rest the myth of the guitar's limited harmonic range.

What I find most interesting about the 12 measures leading to this point is that, as Chopin throws in increasingly remote and discordant harmonies, their full specification becomes less—rather than more—necessary. When the essential meaning of the passage is the fragmentation of tonality, the somewhat smaller fragments of which the guitar is capable become sufficient. There is an intriguing fractal or holographic quality to this phenomenon.

Regarding the melody in this section, as the harmony and tempo become wilder the melodic contour begins to come apart. The eighth-eighth-quarter-quarter figure is thrown up and down into different octaves. The guitar cannot match this range and transposition of some measures is necessary. Although the particular tessitura cannot be matched, the essential feature, if characterized as "fragmentation of the texture," can be conveyed by other means. A likely candidate is the use of boldly contrasting timbre created by alternately playing near the bridge (*ponticello*) and up the neck (*tasto*). By this technique, the transcription substitutes a medium of contrast unavailable to the guitar (wide pitch range) with one that is unavailable to the piano (timbre changes). Transcription often involves discovering this kind of substitution. The task is not to transfer everything from one instrument to another, but rather, to find equivalent, not identical, means of communicating the information or expression.

Measure 72

Transcriptions are instructions for playing on one instrument the music originally written for another. To be complete, these instructions must show what notes to play and, especially on the guitar, how to produce those notes. Now, in addition to the occasional uncertainty about the intended duration of notes, there is a related problem with our notation of fingering: We have no agreed upon method for prescribing how to stop a string from sounding. Indeed, any such notation in guitar scores is exceedingly rare— finger numbers or letters inside parentheses or triangles are the only methods of which I have heard. This is surprising, considering the unsurpassed complexity of fingering fretted instruments as compared to other instruments. On other instruments, ending a note is a trivial issue; on the guitar it can be a puzzle requiring the evaluation of a multitude of possible techniques. Most commonly, it is assumed that a spare left- or right-hand finger or thumb can stop an open string from sounding too long, and in fact that is what I assume the player will often do with the third-beat bass notes on the open fourth and fifth strings throughout the *Nocturne*. There are also other ways of guiding the player to efficient means of stopping notes. Consider measure 72 and 73 (Figure 7).

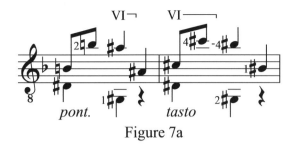

Figure 7a

Figure 7b

This is one spot that I rewrote in my second exploration of the *Nocturne*. The first version is shown in Figure 7b. This seems the most natural as it minimizes movement, but what it implies about note durations is not correct: The barré sign directs the performer to hold the low G sharp, but the quarter rest (and the up-pedal sign in the piano score) indicate that the note should end on the third beat. Perhaps a pianist looking at this would chide us for using contradictory notation! Figure 7a shows that—even absent explicit signs for stopping notes—the transcriber can sometimes, through other means, remind the player of the need to attend to them.

Measure 89–105

The preceding storm of dissonance prepares the way for this utterly calm and consonant episode. It is an extraordinary transition. From the key of G sharp major through a simple, yet magical, transformation, we slip back through the looking glass into entirely familiar surroundings. For the transcriber, as well as the performer, all difficulties fall away.

Measure 106–126

Most Chopin nocturnes return to the opening material, if only in abbreviated form, but this one does not follow that pattern. The melody in octaves is a common pianistic device that is not often preserved in guitar transcriptions. Here, however, except for some of the tied half-notes, the original texture fits well. In performance, the player should take care to dynamically contrast the melody and the accompaniment that surrounds it. Notice that the texture in the original, as in the transcription, has the melody and accompaniment intertwined. Chopin was kind enough to provide no serious obstacles.

Measures 123–126

The top line is moved up an octave to place it in the guitar's sweetest range.

Conclusion

There is wonderful music written originally for the guitar, but most of the best composers—and certainly Frédéric Chopin is in the first rank—channeled their genius to other instruments. Careful and respectful transcription can carry this music to the guitar—not only unharmed but even enhanced—both by the insight the process of transcription gives us into the original music and by the unique and marvelously expressive qualities our instrument offers.

It has been a great pleasure to retrace the journey through this *Nocturne* that I first made several years ago. In doing so I found a few new routes and even changed a few details. I am always interested to hear reactions and comments from people who have played my transcriptions, as this feedback can only improve the results of future projects.

Nocturne

Op. 15, No. 3

Transcribed for guitar
by Richard Yates

Frédéric Chopin
(1810–1849)

I began learning the guitar at about age twelve, in part through a Mel Bay beginners' book. I did not have formal lessons until I was 15, when I studied with Joseph Mayes, and then Peter Collona at the Bryn Mawr Conservatory of Music in Pennsylvania. After graduating from the University of Pennsylvania, I pursued graduate studies at the University of Oregon, and later completed a Master of Science degree at Western Oregon State College. I studied with John Doan at Willamette University for more than ten years. In 1996 I began writing *The Transcriber's Art* for the Guitar Foundation of America's magazine, *Soundboard*, now compiled in this volume. Other collections of my transcriptions feature music by Frédéric Chopin, Edvard Grieg, Edward MacDowell, and Thomas Morley.

Printed in Great Britain
by Amazon